Iqbal Masih
and the
Crusaders
Against
Child Slavery

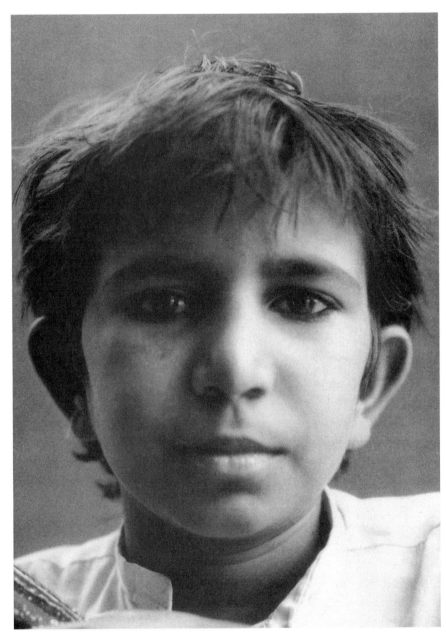

Iqbal Masih

and the Crusaders Against Child Slavery

STOP CHILD SERVITUDE

Susan Kuklin

Henry Holt and Company · New York

Throughout this book I often express the value of the Pakistani, Indian, and Nepali rupees in dollars. Wherever possible I tried to follow the exchange rate at the time in question; this rate fluctuated greatly.

Urdu, and its dialects, is romanized in various ways. I am grateful to Farhad Karim who helped me do this in a uniform manner.

Henry Holt and Company, Inc.
Publishers since 1866
115 West 18th Street
New York, New York 10011

Henry Holt is a registered
trademark of Henry Holt and Company, Inc.

Library of Congress Cataloging-in-Publication Data
Kuklin, Susan.
Iqbal Masih and the crusaders against child slavery / by Susan Kuklin.
p.   cm.
Includes bibliographical references and index.
Summary: An account of the former Pakistani child labor activist whose life and unexplained murder has brought to the attention of the world the evil of child bondage.
1. Masih, Iqbal, 1982–1995—Juvenile literature.   2. Children—Employment—Pakistan—Punjab—Juvenile literature.   3. Rug and carpet industry—Pakistan—Punjab—Employees—Juvenile literature.   4. Children—Employment—Case studies—Juvenile literature.   5. Poor children—Biography—Juvenile literature.   6. Children's rights—Juvenile literature.
[1. Masih, Iqbal, 1982–1995.   2. Children—Employment.   3. Rug and carpet industry—Pakistan.   4. Child abuse.   5. Poor—Biography.   6. Children's rights.]   I. Title.
HD6250.P183P866   1998   331.3'4'092   [B]—DC21   98-5100

ISBN 0-8050-5459-6
First Edition—1998
Printed in the United States of America on acid-free paper. ∞
10   9   8   7   6   5   4   3   2   1

For all the children still waiting to become free,
and for my parents

Contents

Part III – **Reconstruction**

IQBAL MASIH AND
THE CRUSADERS
AGAINST CHILD
SLAVERY

A Note From the Author

A few years ago, the Reebok Human Rights Foundation invited me to Boston to meet an extraordinary young boy by the name of Iqbal Masih. At that time I was in the middle of a series of intense interviews with human rights activists who were visiting New York. I thought to myself, Iqbal is so young and so committed to his cause that there will be plenty of opportunities to talk with him in the future. How wrong can one writer be!

After Iqbal's tragic death, two of his friends and fellow Reebok award winners, Li Lu of China and David Moya of Cuba, asked me to write about Iqbal. The result is this book.

A great deal has been written about Iqbal, child bondage, and the Bonded Labor Liberation Front. Unfortunately, much of the information is inconclusive at best and incorrect at worst. It was perplexing to sort out truth from fiction in the paradoxical life of Iqbal Masih. To this day, there is some question about Iqbal's true age.

To research this book, I spoke with people who either knew Iqbal or met his family. They include Ron Adams, Doug Cahn, Sharon Cohen, Arvind Ganesan, Farhad Karim, Mark Schapiro, and Paula Van Gelder. I also reviewed materials from highly respected human rights organizations. Anti-Slavery International, the Human Rights Commission of Pakistan, Human Rights Watch/Asia, the National Child Labor Committee, and UNICEF provided me with materials about contemporary forms of slavery and the history and background of many of the grassroots organizations that are active in this field.

Iqbal was widely quoted in newspapers, magazines, and videos. More often than not, he repeated the same answers to reporters' questions. Because he worked with many different translators, his descriptions and quotations were slightly different from one source to another. Trudie Styler interviewed Iqbal for the February 1996 issue of *Harper's Bazaar* magazine. It was a wonderful, touching interview called "The Short, Tragic Life of Iqbal Masih." When in doubt, I used Iqbal's quotes from Styler's article.

Two other magazine articles, "Child Labor in Pakistan," by Jonathan Silvers for the *Atlantic Monthly* magazine, February 1996, and "Children of a Lesser God," by

Mark Schapiro for *Harper's Bazaar*, April 1996, gave me invaluable material and insight into this complex topic. They are both worth reading if you want to learn more about child bondage.

I am grateful to all the journalists, researchers, and human rights activists who helped me write this book. My sincere appreciation to my expert readers: Jeannine Guthrie, Farhad Karim, Shalini Dewan, and Ron Adams. Although writing is ultimately a solitary affair, there were a number of friends and colleagues who contributed to this book: Gay Young, my agent; Ian Graham and the wonderful staff at Henry Holt; Sharon Cohen; Paula Van Gelder; and Doug Cahn at the Reebok Human Rights Foundation. My husband, Bailey, provided inspiration, wise counsel, and encouragement. Most especially, I want to thank my editor, Marc Aronson, who supported me through every step and stumble. Together we tried to tell the story of bonded children and to celebrate the life of Iqbal Masih.

I wish with all my heart that this book was not necessary. I wish I had Iqbal here beside me, guiding me through the ins and outs of a now happy life. Even more, I wish that the horrible plight of child bondage no longer existed and that this book would be read as history, not as current events.

A NOTE FROM THE
AUTHOR

Iqbal Masih
and the
Crusaders
Against
Child Slavery

Prologue

I am one of those millions of children who are suffering in Pakistan because of bonded labor and child labor. But I am lucky. Due to the efforts of the Bonded Labor Liberation Front (BLLF), I am free and I am standing in front of you here today. After I was freed, I joined the BLLF school. I am studying in that school now. For us slave children, Eshan Ullah Khan and BLLF has done the same work that Abraham Lincoln did for the slaves in America. Today you are free and I am free, too.

Unfortunately, the owner of the business where I worked told us that it is America who asks us to enslave the children. American people like the cheap carpets, the rugs, and the towels that we make. So they want bonded labor to go on. I appeal to you that you stop people from using children as bonded laborers because the children need to use a pen rather than the instruments of child labor.

Children work with this instrument. [Iqbal holds up a carpet tool.] *If there is something wrong, the children get beaten with it. And if they are hurt, they are not taken to the doctors. Children do not need these instruments but they need this instrument, the pen, like the American children have.* [He holds up a pen.] *Unfortunately, many children do not use pens right now. I hope that you will help BLLF, just as they have helped us. By your cooperation BLLF can help a lot of children and give them this instrument, the pen.*

I share what I remember: how I was abused and how other children are being abused there, including those that are insulted, and are hung upside down, and are mistreated. I still remember those days.

I saw Pakistani-made rugs in American stores, and I was very saddened knowing that they were made by bonded labor children. I felt very sorry about it. I request President Clinton to put sanctions on those countries which use child labor. Do not extend help to those countries still using children as bonded laborers. Allow the children to have the pen.

And with this I gratefully and thankfully acknowledge Reebok's contribution in that direction. They have called me for this prize, and I'm very grateful to them. Thank you.

We have a slogan at school when children are freed. We all together say we are free. And I request you to join me today in raising that slogan here. I will say, "We are," and you will say, "Free."

—IQBAL MASIH, 1994

The slight young boy from the other side of the world raised both his arms triumphantly. "WE ARE," he shouted. His cry, both fragile and powerful, energized two thousand voices.

"FREE," the voices screamed. "FREE! FREE! FREE!"

In response to the audience's chant, his impish smile lit up the stage. Pakistani-born Iqbal Masih was addressing an audience at

Iqbal accepting Reebok's
"Youth in Action" Award

*Courtesy of Richard
Sobel/Reebok Human Rights
Foundation*

Northeastern University, in Boston. He was in America to receive the Reebok Human Rights Youth in Action Award. Just the fact that he was there, standing before the crowd, was a stunning accomplishment.

At one time, Iqbal Masih was destined to spend his entire life tucked away in a tiny factory, weaving carpets. Instead he emerged to become an international speaker and award winner.

Iqbal Masih was one of the millions of children all over the world who fill their days working to help their impoverished families pay off debts or eke out a small living. Most indentured children work at home, on farms, or in dangerous jobs such as street hawking, brick breaking, and ragpicking. Some children weave carpets. Others sew clothing and solder jewelry. Some make toys and sporting equipment. Others grind metal surgical tools, such as syringes. These and other products are then exported abroad, especially to Europe and the United States. Not all exported goods are made by the sweat and exploitation of children. UNICEF reports that only a small amount of exported goods, about 5 percent, are made by working young people.

Most of the young workers portrayed in this book are called "debt-bonded laborers." They are sold to employers or agents in return for a small loan. They do not go to school. They have very little time to play with friends. Many do not even live near their families. International law calls this kind of transaction a "contemporary form of slavery."

This is a true story about a boy who went from slavery to freedom, about many other children who are still enslaved, and about what people, both young and older, can do to stop child bondage. To bring about change, we first have to understand the roots of the problem. It is not unique to the modern developing world. Child slavery and child labor have a long history in America and Europe as well.

WHO SELLS THEIR CHILDREN?

Very poor families are often faced with a terrible choice: sell a child into bondage and eat, or keep everyone together and starve. One farm mother told a reporter why she sold her son into bondage. "If I had enough grains from the land, enough water and food—would I not gather all my children and keep them close to me? . . . Why would I send them away? It is my helplessness, my poverty."

Some parents do not know about the terrible conditions where their children work. Others are very much aware of the difficult time in store for their children, but they are desperate—there is little they can do.

Families with working children might have more food on their tables, perhaps better roofs on their houses. But for the most part they remain poor, landless, and with little hope for a brighter future. Their lives are harsh. They have few opportunities to offer their children a decent education.

THE GLOBAL MARKET

Many poor children of South Asia—India, Pakistan, Nepal, Bangladesh, and Sri Lanka—work alongside their families. They help out in the fields and do chores in the home. The more these families need money, not just helping hands, the more children are viewed as an inexpensive resource. The family has no choice but to turn their young children into laborers. These children have no power and few allies. Though local human rights groups try to protect them from the worst abuses, few people in power pay attention. If this problem is due to weak or callous governments in developing countries, it is also due to greedy companies in rich ones.

Recently many industries that do business around the world—large companies that export such items as clothing, sporting equipment, and carpets—have moved their factories to poor countries or hired local workers to produce their merchandise. They commonly choose countries that do not have, or do not enforce, strict labor laws. They look the other way as children are hired to do adult work.

From the employer's point of view, hiring children makes good economic sense. Children work for less money than adults. They are submissive and unlikely to organize or protest. The lower production prices are passed along to the customer.

The selling of handmade carpets, made by children like Iqbal Masih, is a prime example. Consumers all over the world are eager for bargains. Stores in the United States and Europe can no longer buy carpets made in Iran because there is a boycott in place. During the time Iqbal wove carpets, Afghanistan, another country famous for handmade carpets, was in the middle of a war with the Soviet Union. Merchants and exporters from countries in South Asia jumped in to fill the void. They were able to provide consumers with inexpensive carpets, jewelry, sports equipment, and clothing. There are few expenses: materials and labor, which are fairly cheap, and, in some cases, bribe money, which is negotiable.

International trade flourishes; the marketplace is global. This puts children in poor countries at ever greater risk. Yet the new connections that link people across the seas have also brought the terrible exploitation of these youngsters to the world's attention. If we want to enjoy the fruits of the global marketplace, we also have to accept global responsibilities.

The media, faxes, and the Internet can bring news into our homes with the press of a button. As a result, human rights monitors and journalists are able to tell us chilling stories about exploited children working in both large cities and remote villages. A number of these reports are included in this book.

Although an enormous number of working children are from South Asia, this problem is worldwide. UNICEF's 1997 report *The State of the World's Children* claims that "children work all over the world, in both industrialized and developing countries, although it is in the developing world that most child labor takes place." Because Iqbal Masih was from Pakistan, he was able to tell us what was happening in his country. Pakistan is just one of the many countries that uses children to do adult work.

There are no easy answers to the problem of bonded child labor. On the one hand, the laws that protect these children must be enforced. On the other hand, as we will see, for the international community to ban child labor can lead to dreadful consequences. Poor families only become more desperate. Children and their parents have to be provided with useful alternatives: children need meaningful educations and adults need jobs with acceptable working conditions at sufficient wages.

Iqbal Masih has become a symbol of the many children who work as modern-day slaves. He and the other freed young people who speak out in these pages were helped along the way by human rights activists—modern-day abolitionists who are committed to the emancipation of exploited children.

Iqbal's road to freedom and fame was truly remarkable. It started twelve years before his visit to Boston. . . .

Part I
Modern-Day Slaves and the New Abolitionists

Chapter 1
My Name Is Iqbal

I started working when I was four. I used to leave my home at four in the morning and come back at seven at night.

—IQBAL MASIH

It is brutally hot in Muridke, a small village deep in the heart of Punjab. The village is made up of clay dwellings, each protected by high, earthen-colored walls. Naked toddlers romp in an irrigation ditch, while water buffalo languish in its coolness. Young girls wash their family's clothing on the rocks along the bank.

The men of the village, wearing traditional *shalwaar kamiz,* baggy cotton trousers and long shirts, sip tea and gossip at the local *dera,* or meeting place. Hidden behind the earthen walls, young wives suckle their newborns and clean the homes that they share with their in-laws.

In this sun-scorched village lived Saif Masih and his wife, Inayat Bibi. (In Pakistan women are often called by their given name followed by the word *bibi,* which means "dear woman.") They were very poor. At times there was barely enough money to feed their growing family. Inayat eked out a living as a housecleaner. Some say that Saif, a laborer, had a drug problem and was not a reliable wage earner. On top of that, the Masihs were Christian. *Masih* means "messiah" in Pakistan's national language, Urdu. Many Christians in Pakistan have the surname Masih. In Pakistan, Christians tend to be a minority who often face discrimination.

Inayat Bibi and her
daughter in an undated
photo

Courtesy of Mark Schapiro

The family lived in a two-room house within a walled courtyard. On hot nights they slept outside, in the courtyard, on a large *charpay,* a bed or platform made of hemp. Hanging beneath the *charpay* was a hammock made of cloth that acted as a crib for the newest baby.

In 1982 a baby boy was born to Inayat Bibi and Saif Masih. They named him Iqbal. Iqbal Masih.

Sometime after Iqbal's birth, Saif Masih deserted the family. While Iqbal's mother worked, his older sisters took care of him and his other siblings.

Iqbal did not go to school. Education was not compulsory nor widely available in Pakistan. Very few poor children learn to read and write. He spent his earliest years playing in the fields until he was ready to help his family by going to work.

By 1986 an older son of Saif Masih was about to be married. The celebration would include feasting and processions. Weddings are very important to the people of Pakistan. Wedding celebrations are often held even if a person is short of money or out of work. Saif Masih was no exception. He knew that as father of the groom, he must pay for part of the festivities, even though he had deserted his family.

Like most poor laborers, Saif was never able to save much. No bank would give him a loan. He could not apply to the government for aid because there were few programs to help poor people. People such as Iqbal's father are forced to turn to local moneylenders, local employers, or landlords to get the money they need.

In Muridke, many poor people simply borrow from a local *thekedar*, an employer who owns a nearby carpet factory. In return for the loan, the employer expects collateral, a guarantee of something of value to secure the loan. Saif Masih's only valuable possessions were his children.

Saif asked Iqbal's uncle to contact the *thekedar*. The *thekedar* was willing—probably only too happy—to lend Saif money. In return, one of Saif's children would go to work in this fast-growing business. Iqbal, a scrappy four-year-old, was considered ready to work.

The uncle borrowed 600 rupees (approximately $12) from the contractor. Little Iqbal would weave carpets until all the money, including an undisclosed amount of interest and expenses, was paid back. This transaction is called a *peshgi*, a loan, and it ended Iqbal's childhood forever. From that day forward, Iqbal became a "debt-bonded laborer."

As were the slaves in America about 150 years earlier, bonded workers are attached to their master. (Iqbal referred to the *thekedar* as "carpet master.") The master has all the power in the relationship; the bonded laborers have none. Workers cannot change jobs. They cannot refuse work. They are at the whim of their employer all day, every day. In many cases, the entire family of the bonded worker is subject to the master as well. Any form of resistance or protest can be met with severe punishment, including beatings and torture.

Unlike the American slaves of yesteryear, bonded labor is not an official policy of the government. It is illegal. The constitution of Pakistan, for instance, absolutely forbids slavery. Slavery, especially the slave labor of children, is illegal throughout the world, and there are international laws to protect poor workers. Unfortunately these laws are not always enforced.

Modern slave labor in Pakistan and other countries is not based on the color of one's skin. It is based on the exploitation of a person's poverty. The laborers do not necessarily come from another place, as did the American slaves from Africa, though large numbers of bonded laborers all over the world are migrants from other countries. Contemporary slaves are not sold in an open marketplace, and there are no ownership papers. Bondage continues because of indifference and greed.

. . .

When Iqbal began his bondage, the *peshgi* was widespread among the poor people in South Asia. Poor, landless, rural families, with little or no schooling, are not likely to escape from the brutal system of work-for-loans. Bonded labor is a way of life for many children in many countries.

One mother told a reporter, "When my children were three, I told them they must be prepared to work for the good of the family. I told them again and again that they would be bonded at five. And when the time came for them to go, they were prepared and went without complaint."

Under the terms of the *peshgi*, Iqbal was to weave carpets six days a week, twelve hours a day, until he worked off the 600-rupee loan. His training, the tools that he used, and the food that he ate were additional expenses. If he made mistakes while weaving the intricate designs, he would be fined. In order to learn the art of carpet weaving, Iqbal would spend a year or so as an apprentice. During this period, he would not be paid.

Since it is illegal to sell a child in Pakistan, there was no written agreement between the *thekedar* and Iqbal's uncle. Only the *thekedar* would keep a record of the expenses that would be added to the *peshgi*. If the *thekedar* chose to pad the bill, there was no way to challenge him. There were no witnesses. No contract. Just a simple handshake and Iqbal belonged to the carpet master.

Iqbal was not present while his "sale" was taking place. Later that evening he was told that he was going to work in the nearby carpet factory. No questions. No discussion. Tradition dictates that children do not question their elders, just as wives do not question their husbands. An obedient child, Iqbal obeyed the wishes of his father. The following morning he went to work.

HOW TO BUY A CHILD

Selling Iqbal into bondage was a straightforward transaction. In other cases, buying children is more involved. Let's say an exporter decides to sell some rugs. He contacts a store in Europe or America that is willing to pay $500 each for fifty rugs. If he does not have his own factory, he usually hires a contractor to get the job done. Some exporters do not even know who actually makes their carpets. Often the exporter will set up a business arrangement with the contractor. "Get me fifty rugs in six months, and I will pay you $250 for each one." The contractor then says to a middleman, or subcontractor, "Get me fifty rugs in six months, and I will pay $125 for each of them." The subcontractor swings into action. He calls on his network of recruiting agents, watching agents, and conveying agents.

Recruiting agents travel to remote villages and make contact with watching agents. The watching agent is usually a person who lives in the village and knows which families are experiencing tough times. The watching agent introduces the recruiting agent to the head of a needy household. The recruiter pretends to be concerned about the plight of the family. He offers his help. "I will place your child in a company where he will learn a trade."

The needy family has little choice. A deal is made, and the child is handed over to a conveying agent, who then takes the new child laborer to the factory. The child now belongs to the factory owner.

People must be paid for their services. Some of the middlemen are not much wealthier than the laborers they seek to enslave. And everyone, everyone, answers to the person higher up on the chain of command. Some of the agents and employers are decent enough and treat the children kindly. Others are very cruel. None of the children are paid properly for their hard labor.

IQBAL, THE APPRENTICE

Iqbal's job at the carpet factory was essentially no different from that of millions of other young people who work day and night to help their families. At four o'clock in the morning, he was picked up by the *thekedar* and driven to the factory where he was to work the next six years of his life. He was put in an airless room, big enough for about twenty looms. A small, bare lightbulb gave out little light. It was sticky and hot inside the room because all the windows were sealed tight to keep out any insects that might damage the wool.

Iqbal took his place in front of a large wooden carpet loom. He was to squat on a small rutted wood platform. (In some factories children sit on cushions. Other factories have trenches dug into the floor to hold the looms in place. The weavers sit on a plank with their legs dangling into a trench. These trenches also provide sleeping places for the children who work far from their families.) Large balls of colored wool were hung near the loom. Red, blue, purple, green—colored thread that would become gorgeous flowers, majestic trees, exotic birds, and sophisticated geometric designs. The *ustaad*, teacher, explained the process called "knotting."

WARP AND WEFT

A loom ready for weaving is simply a wooden frame fastened vertically with white strands of wool. The vertical strands of wool, the "warp" of

Bonded children weaving carpets

Courtesy of Mats Öhman/Bergmar Productions

the rug, act as a skeleton or anchor. Iqbal was taught how to pull the colored thread from the large balls and tie tiny knots around each white warp.

The rows and rows of horizontal knots, called the "weft" of the carpet, must be cut at exactly the same thickness, or else the pile of the rug will be bumpy and uneven.

Like all the other children at the factory, Iqbal learned how to use sharp instruments to tie and tighten the weft's innumerable knots. Once a line of knots was complete, he used a "beating comb," an object with metal blades that look like teeth, to tighten the lines. He clipped the wool evenly with a sharp knife. It was a complicated, monotonous job, and if the young apprentice did not pay careful attention, the blades could cut deeply into his flesh.

The intricate design is created by following the *naksha,* a paper map, which shows where each colored wool is placed. This is how beautiful carpets are made.

"NIMBLE FINGERS"

It takes about six months for a trained weaver to tie the million or so knots that make the most intricate four-by-six-foot carpets. Carpets with smaller, more dense knots are more valuable than the ones that are thicker and more loosely spaced. Some carpet manufacturers claim that workers with tiny fingers can make smaller knots. Those with the smallest, most nimble fingers are, of course, young children. Elsewhere children's nimble fingers plunge into scalding water and carefully unravel silk threads loosened from their boiling cocoons. Their nimble fingers solder delicate silver flowers to necklaces and bracelets. Their nimble fingers sew soccer balls. Nimble fingers make bricks and roll cheap cigarettes called *beedis.*

Human rights researchers report that this is a myth. Children make the poorer quality, less expensive goods. "Nimble fingers" is but one of many reasons employers give for turning children into modern-day slaves.

Bonded carpet laborers
and their *naksha*

Courtesy of Farhad Karim

In the beginning, it was hard for Iqbal to learn to sit still for so many long hours because he had been such an active child. To ensure that he would not run away, a *chowkidar,* a guard or watch person, chained Iqbal to his loom for hours at a time. The *chowkidar* was always present, always watching, to be certain that the children were working.

Chapter 2
Carpet Weavers

We were too frightened to help each other.

—IQBAL MASIH

When Iqbal completed his work as an apprentice, he was then ready to weave carpets. He worked beside twenty other boys. His earnings amounted to one rupee a day (two cents), even though he worked from four o'clock in the morning until seven that evening.

The children in the shop were not allowed to speak to one another. "If the children spoke, they were not giving their complete attention to the product and were liable to make errors," Iqbal later told journalists. Many other freed laborers told similar stories.

Lint and fluff floated in the air. Iqbal would breathe it in and cough it out. Sweat poured down Iqbal's face as he leaned close to the loom. The *thekedar* screamed, "Don't soil the wool!"

At night he was driven back to his family. He was too tired to play his favorite sport, cricket. "I didn't have time to play ball," he explained later. It didn't take long for the bounce to fade from Iqbal's walk.

Iqbal and his fellow weavers were warned never to leave the factory during working hours. "If we tried to escape, we were threatened with being thrown in boiling oil," he said. "If we were slow, we often got lashed on our backs and heads."

Concentration was crucial. Mistying a single knot led to fines or beatings. Daydreaming could have serious consequences. The sharp, crescent-shaped weavers' tool would slip and nick his fingers. This happened many times.

Once, when Iqbal was so exhausted he began to doze off, the sharp knife slid, digging into the flesh of his forefinger. "Hold your hand up!" the *thekedar* shouted. "Don't let the blood drip!" The carpet master did not want Iqbal's blood to stain the precious wool thread. To stop the bleeding, the carpet master dripped hot oil onto the wound. The oil, used to seal the wound, stung horribly and Iqbal screamed. His screams were answered with a slap on the head and an order to get back to work.

Every afternoon the laborers were given a half-hour lunch break. Iqbal said, "We were kept hungry." The *thekedar* provided the youngsters a small portion of rice and lentils. Sometimes there would be a few other vegetables added to the meal. The cost of this simple meal was immediately added to the children's *peshgi,* increasing their debt.

The cramped, overheated conditions inside such factories often lead to disease. Weavers inhaling thousands of tiny wool fibers can get emphysema or tuberculosis. Many suffer from scabies and skin ulcers because of the "constant exposure to the wool." More often than not, their posture is bowed because they are forced to squat on the wooden platform for long hours. Their hands ache with carpal tunnel syndrome and arthritis.

Iqbal said, "We weren't allowed many days off. Even sick children were not allowed to rest." If a child weaver complained that he was too sick to work, the *chowkidar* locked him in a dark closet known as the punishment room. "They also hung children upside down until they became sicker. Children were beaten," said Iqbal.

Although most bonded children are docile and obedient, there are a few who are not afraid to talk back. These young people are often hit, chained to their looms, or locked in dark, musty closets. Iqbal was one of the "talk back" boys. He was beaten more often than the other children because, time and time again, he defied the master. He spoke up when he thought something was not right. "Sometimes I was fined."

In a way, the fines were worse than the beatings. They raised Iqbal's debt higher and higher. Instead of paying off his bondage, he was increasing the time it would take to earn his freedom.

In factories similar to the one where Iqbal worked, children are battered for all kinds of infractions. One young boy was not a good weaver, and the *chowkidar* constantly hit him with a stick. A researcher reports, "Once, after he made a terrible mistake, the foreman took a shearing knife and made a deep cut between Salim's thumb and index finger. The boy was so terrified of the foreman that he did not dare register a complaint."

WORKING GIRLS

Most bonded girls have a tougher time than the boys. They are paid even less and are exposed to all kinds of sexual abuse. In addition,

Bonded girl weaving
a carpet

Courtesy of Farhad Karim

after working long hours to earn money, girls have to help inside the home. They take care of their siblings, clean the house, wash the clothing, shop at the market, and cook dinner. At an evening education center, a human rights researcher asked one group of child laborers "what they did for fun." The boys said that they played with their friends, they went to the movies, and they rode their bicycles. The girls did not understand the question. Their teacher explained that "the girls do not have the opportunity to do anything for fun; when they are not working for wages or against a loan, they are working for the family."

Despite these hardships, some young girls say that they see bondage as a chance to make money and leave the drudgery of village life. Gauri Maya Taming, a carpet weaver in Kathmandu, the capital of Nepal, was tired of taking care of her eight brothers and sisters. She was excited at the chance of going to the big city and working at a "proper" job.

Our family has a tiny plot of land in a village near Hetauda, a ten-hour bus ride from Kathmandu. We never had enough to eat and we children used to help with the housework and the work in the field. I had to gather firewood and fodder [coarse food for cattle], look after the babies, plant, weed and harvest the field, and graze the cattle.

I was eleven years old when a man from our village told my parents that I could earn good money weaving carpets in Kathmandu. I was so excited: not only about going to the capital but because I would escape the hardship of life at home. My parents were happy to let me go because some girls from our village had become weavers in Kathmandu and were already sending money home.

I was trained in the factory for three months before I started work. At that time, like all the other trainees, I was not paid but I was given food and a place to sleep. That was the toughest time. It's hard to move your fingers between the taut threads of a loom, as it makes them numb. I'm used to it now but it's still painful work.

I get backaches and coughs. In winter my hands get dry and it's painful to work at the loom. Sometimes, I have fever and treat it myself with medicine I buy from the local pharmacy.

I get paid about Rs. 500 [$17] a month. I and two other friends work at one loom and produce about two carpets, 15 feet by 16 feet, a month.

IQBAL MASIH AND
THE CRUSADERS
AGAINST CHILD
SLAVERY

Gauri Maya Taming, a car-
pet weaver in Kathmandu

*Courtesy of Anti-Slavery
International*

We've heard that the carpets we weave are sold in foreign countries at more than Rs. 10,000 [*about $350*] each.

I know that I'm not paid enough. I share a room with five other girls. Each of us pays Rs. 50 [*$2*] but on top of that, we have to buy food, fuel, clothes, and medicine. There isn't much left to save. What there is, I keep at the factory. My father comes from the village every four months or so and collects whatever is there.

I've not been home since I started here, two years ago. Life is easier and I enjoy the company of my friends. We go to the cinema now and then. I suppose I'd like to go home, but only when I'm rich. My father said that he'll bring my younger sister here this autumn. It will be nice to have my sister here. We can support our family together.

Journalist Jonathan Silvers reports that bondage is so common, many children consider it an event that will change them into adults. He interviewed twelve-year-old Irfana, who said, "My friends and I knew that sooner or later we'd be sent off to the factories or the fields. We were tired of doing chores and minding infants. We looked forward to the day when we'd be given responsibilities and the chance to earn money. At the time, work seemed glamorous and children who worked seemed quite important."

Irfana found out soon enough just how unglamorous her life was to be. She continued, "My master bought, sold, and traded us like livestock, and sometimes he shipped us great distances. The boys were beaten frequently to make them work long hours. The girls were often violated. My best friend got ill after she was raped, and when she couldn't work, the master sold her to a friend of his in a village a thousand kilometers away. Her family was never told where she was sent, and they never saw her again."

The most exploited children work far from their families. Many of them are given little food and no clean clothing. They sleep inside the factory or in a nearby shed. The doors and windows are locked to keep the children from escaping. In many cases, when they make mistakes, complain, or even simply ask about their parents, they are beaten, tortured, or abused.

THE CARPET CHILDREN OF THAR

Thar is a sprawling desert in southern Pakistan. There are few roads, just sandy tracts that weave throughout the district. The brackish waters from the wells are unsafe for drinking. Tuberculosis and malaria run rampant. The main activity in this region is smuggling. Travelers and tourists are definitely not welcome. A Canadian human rights researcher visited Thar as part of an ongoing investigation into bonded labor. In the middle of the night, he and a local activist sneaked into a compound that was surrounded by a high, stucco wall. Behind the wall were a group of young boys making carpets. He said, "The compound seemed nicer than the urban factories I had visited earlier because it is in the open air."

Their *chowkidar* was not in the compound, so the weavers were eager to talk. Some were confident young people, while others were a little shy. The researcher said, "You don't see these young people and think, 'Wow, they are so different.' That's what makes it even more compelling. They are kids, just like here."

The children understood exactly why they were working. One boy explained, "My parents were given money, and I'm here to apprentice." Another said that he worked there because his mother needed money for some kind of emergency, though he didn't know what kind. "When I was eight, my mother pledged me to the carpet contractor for 5,000 rupees [*$150*]." The boy was then taken to this desert carpet-weaving center, where he worked and slept. Occasionally he was given permission to spend a night or two at his home with his mother. Like so many others, he knotted carpets twelve to sixteen hours a day, six or seven days a week. He was given some food, a little free time, and no medical care. He was told that he could not stop working until he earned enough money to repay a family debt. If he made a mistake, he was fined. If he worked too slowly, he was beaten with a stick. The *thekedar* kept increasing the debt by claiming that he had additional expenses because he was looking after the boy. As the debt increased, it became virtually impossible to repay it. By the time he met the Canadian monitor, he was nineteen years old and still trying to pay off the debt.

. . .

One by one, the boys at the carpet center told the monitor their grievances. The boys never complained about working; they complained about their conditions. "They are mean to us . . . they beat us . . . they yell at us . . . they curse us."

They told the Canadian how they would cut themselves with the carpet tools to get a little time off. And they told him about the time a few of them ran away. When the *chowkidar* who guarded them dozed off, the boys scaled the wall and began running. They raced to a nearby house and asked for help. The owner of the house said that it was too dangerous for him to hide the powerful employer's workers. There was nowhere to go and no one to help them, so they set off into the desert.

Walking, walking, walking into the night, they had no idea where they were. At least they were free.

Finally a car approached. It was the *chowkidar*. "Get in!" he barked. They climbed into the car and returned to the compound. Once inside, they were savagely beaten. The following day the badly bruised children went back to work.

KIDNAPPING

We wept and pleaded with Panna Lal to let us go back to our parents.
—SURAJ, A SEVEN-YEAR-OLD
BOY FROM INDIA

A very young boy was playing near his home in a village in the northwestern part of Pakistan. Someone drove up, snatched him, and sold him to a carpet center far away from his family. The boy was told that he would not be freed until he repaid the price of his debt.

Unfortunately this kidnapping is not an isolated incident. Anti-Slavery International, the world's oldest international human rights organization, has released a harrowing report about children who were kidnapped and sold into slavery. A local barber in a small town in

India told a group of young boys that he would take them to the movies in another town. But first they had to promise not to tell their parents where they were going. Excited about seeing a film, they solemnly pledged not to tell anyone. Instead of going to the movies, the barber drove them to a remote village in another state and sold them into bondage.

At first the boys were locked up and beaten. They continued to be beaten whenever they asked for food, whenever they asked where they were, or whenever they cried for their parents. Their day began at 4 A.M. when their owner, Panna Lal, woke them up by pouring cold water over them. They worked until lunch. For lunch they were fed *roti*, an Indian flat bread, and some lentils. Then they were forced to work until midnight. Needless to say, many of the youngsters became ill. There was no medicine, no doctor. Seven boys tried to run away but were caught and viciously punished.

It was two months before an Indian human rights group called the Bonded Liberation Front (BLF) was able to force the police to make an investigation. The children were freed and reunited with their parents. The barber was arrested. He told the police that he sold the children into bondage because he needed money for a new motorbike. Very soon thereafter, he was released on bail. Panna Lal, the master who had so tortured the children, was never prosecuted at all.

There are still many young people just like Iqbal who weave carpets every day. But carpet weaving is not the only form of child bondage. Ashiq makes bricks. Sumathi and Velayulhan roll *beedis*. Selvakumar makes silver jewelry. Some children work at home alongside their families while others, like Gauri Maya, work very far away.

These children, most of whom are newly freed, talked with monitors and reporters about their bondage. They speak out for other, voiceless, faceless children who continue to toil in factories, fields, homes, mines, and shops.

Chapter 3
Modern Forms of Slavery

I am very sad that my father died; so is my mother. Whenever I go to work for the agent he scolds me. I am very sad with my life.

—MUNIRATHNA, A TWELVE-YEAR-OLD GIRL FROM INDIA WHO WAS SOLD INTO SLAVERY AFTER HER FATHER DIED

THE BRICKMAKERS

My name is Ashiq. I am an eleven-year-old boy working in the brick kilns for the past six years. My place of work is on the Grand Trunk

Born a bonded slave at a brick kiln in Pakistan

Courtesy of Mats Öhman/ Bergmar Productions

Road, outside Lahore, near Wagah Border. Along with me, my father and elder brother also work there. My father had taken a loan of 20,000 rupees [*approximately $600*] for the marriage of my sister. It had accumulated to 25,000 rupees [*approximately $750*] within a period of two years. The brick kiln owner deducted from our wages about 15 percent of payment toward the refund of debt. Our daily earnings came to 70 rupees [*$2.10*], but only if we completed 1,000 bricks. I went to school only for three months. Due to pressure from the owner, my father brought me back from school, and I began work on the *bhatta*. We go to work around 2 A.M., when it is still dark, and return by 6 P.M., after sunset. We have a short rest of half an hour from 8 to 8:30 A.M. I am given no time to play. One-day holiday in a month has been given to me. My hope is to enjoy freedom, if I am released from bondage, so that I may learn about some other trade in a better way. . . . With my father, brother (fifteen years old), and sister (eight), we are able to earn about 500 rupees [*about $15*] a week.

At brick kilns entire families work from the early morning hours to late at night. Working barefoot, they are exposed often to the blistering sun in the summertime and freezing cold in the winter. Throughout the day they inhale fine dust particles from the clay.

To make a simple brick, dirt from around a brick kiln area is dug up to be combined with water. This compound is the basic ingredient of bricks. *Patheras,* workers in wet clay, shape the mixture into a brick mold. The *katcha,* raw bricks, are later taken to the kiln by another set of workers, usually adult men.

According to a report by Human Rights Watch/Asia, "A family can prepare approximately 1,000 *katcha* bricks per day." They are usually paid between 80 and 110 rupees ($2.40 and $3.30) per 1,000 bricks produced. Those same bricks are sold at the market for 1,300 rupees ($39). Workers are guarded by hired *chowkidars* or by their employers. If they need to go away from the brick site for any reason, they have to leave either a family member as hostage or a "material possession" as a guarantee that they will return. If a worker tries to file a complaint with the police, he is usually laughed at, abused, and returned to the kiln.

THE *BEEDI* ROLLER

My father and mother force me to go to work with the agent. The agent often beats me. If I tell my father, he allows me to stay home the following day, but then they are pushing me to go again. My father and mother say I have to go. I don't want to go. I am afraid of my agent. But my parents force me to go; if I don't go they scold me and beat me.

Every week the agent gives my wages to my parents. If it is less money than usual, they beat me.

In my family there are seven members, so it is difficult to even get enough food to eat. That's why my father goes to the agent—to ask for more money. But the agent won't give it, because he says I don't work hard enough. But every day I am being sent back to the agent.

—SUMATHI, A TWELVE-YEAR-OLD
GIRL FROM INDIA, BONDED TO
ROLL *BEEDIS* WHEN SHE WAS SEVEN

Children who roll *beedis* spend their days sitting cross-legged on a dirt floor with straw baskets, filled with loose tobacco and a stack of rolling papers, on their laps. The roller puts tobacco onto the paper, rolls it up tightly, and ties it with string. The tips of the cigarette are customarily closed by a younger child who is just beginning to work as a *beedi* roller.

Most of the children are taught to keep their heads tucked down to their chests so that they will roll and tie the *beedis* quickly. "Most of the older children—those over ten—roll 1,500 to 2,000 *beedis* a day."

Fourteen-year-old M. Saritha told a UNICEF representative, "If we were late, they'd beat us. They said, 'Why are you not rolling the *beedis* well? Why are they so big and so few? Don't look up, look down and roll *beedis*.' If we rolled them fast, our hands ached, our necks ached, our backs ached from hunching over."

As with the brick kiln workers, a guard keeps watch over the bonded *beedi* laborers, screaming or smacking them if they don't work fast enough. Human rights monitors have seen some cases where children are forced to sit with a matchbox under their chins so that they will keep their heads tucked downward and concentrate on their work.

MODERN FORMS OF
SLAVERY

IQBAL MASIH AND
THE CRUSADERS
AGAINST CHILD
SLAVERY

A girl in India rolling
beedis (cigarettes)

M. Velayulhan worked at his job for eight years. He told a UNICEF representative what life was like rolling 2,000 *beedis* a day for less than fifty cents. "I would go to the agent's house at eight o'clock in the morning and work till one o'clock. I had an hour to eat, then he'd keep me working till nine o'clock at night. By then, my hands and nose were all blistered and burned from the stench. I was always coughing."

SILVERSMITHS

> *Very small pieces* [of silver] *have to be placed in very small and precise spots. We used a small wire for this job, like a bicycle spoke. Sometimes the owner would beat me with this hot wire if he thought I wasn't working properly. He would take the wire and beat me on the arms.*
>
> —SELVAKUMAR, AGE TWELVE

Selvakumar began working as a silversmith in India when he was eight years old. His parents sold him for a 3,000-rupee ($85) advance because he was "not studying properly." He was taught to solder tiny silver flowers and screws to earrings.

Once he was free, living in a home for street children, Selvakumar talked with a human rights monitor about his bondage. He said that after three years he ran away from the factory, but his "older brother found him and brought him back." The second time he ran away, he went to a shelter for street children. When the owner found him, the shelter's director would not give him back. Then Selvakumar's mother went to the shelter, had him released, and returned him to the factory. The third time he ran away, he refused to return to his parents' house.

The human rights monitor also interviewed another twelve-year-old, Manojan. The monitor reported that Manojan worked with "a crude blowtorch, welding together the tiny silver links and decorations of bracelets and necklaces. He had no mask to protect him from the flame, and his eyes teared continuously from staring at the junction of flame and fine metal pieces. He earned 10 rupees [*about 28 cents*] a day."

Manojan sang a song for the monitor. He learned it at the education center where he was interviewed.

My mother is crying;
I am working in a silver smithy at the age of six.
When I went to school the teacher opposed me—
"You can't study here! Go home!"
Now I am as if blind.
You send me to the factory because we are poor.
But we will always be poor.
You send me to the factory to earn a regular income.
But instead of regular income, I carry the heavy burden of a loan.
This loan burden is my poison.

Ashiq, Sumathi, Velayulhan, and Selvakumar are four of the many children who provided human rights researchers and reporters with firsthand reports about modern child slavery. As more information about exploited and abused bonded children became known, Jonathan Silvers asked Shabbir Jamal, an adviser to Pakistan's Ministry of Labor, how his government could excuse bonded child labor. He answered, "Westerners conveniently forget their own shameful histories when they come here. . . . Europeans addressed slavery and child labor only after they became prosperous. Pakistan has only now entered an era of economic stability that will allow us to expand our horizons and address social concerns."

Myths About Bonded Children

Myth: Children must be trained at the "right" age or they will never learn a skill.

Myth: Children must be trained in a profession "appropriate" to their background or class.

Myth: Children are well suited for certain kinds of work because of their nimble fingers.

Myth: Child labor is a natural and inevitable function of the family unit.

Shabbir Jamal was referring to the turn of the twentieth century, when thousands of underage, poor, usually immigrant children worked in the factories, mills, mines, and farms throughout the United States and Great Britain. Their experiences were remarkably similar to those of Iqbal and other contemporary child slaves.

Child labor is part of the history of the United States. Now it is no longer necessary to employ many children. (But some children—ethnic minorities, immigrants, and migrant workers—still work long hours for less than the legal minimum wage.) Is it fair that people who live comfortably in the wealthy, developed countries point a finger at the working conditions of poorer, developing countries? Should people in glass houses throw stones?

Chapter 4
Glass Houses

I sold my farm and stock, paid up all my debts, and moved my family to a cotton mill. . . . Now my youngest daughter, only 14 years old, is making $6 per week, my other two are making $7.50 each per week and my two boys are making $8 per week and I am making $4.50 per week.

—FROM A HANDBILL DISTRIBUTED
BY A COTTON MILL EMPLOYER IN
NORTH CAROLINA, 1907

Frederick K. Brown wrote (under the pen name Al Priddy) about his childhood labor in the 1890s in a cotton mill:

Five days of the week, at the outer edge of winter, I never stood out in the daylight. I was a human mole, going to work while the stars were out and returning home under the stars. . . . The sun rose and set on the wide world outside, rose and set five times a week, but I might as well have been in a grave; there was no exploration abroad.

The mule-room [*spinning room*] atmosphere was kept at from eighty-five to ninety degrees of heat. The hard wood floor burned my bare feet. I had to gasp quick, short gasps to get air into my lungs at all. My face seemed swathed in continual fire. The tobacco chewers expectorated on the floor, and left little pools for me to wade through. Oil and hot grease dripped down behind the mules [*machinery*], sometimes falling on my scalp or making yellow splotches on my overalls or feet. Under the excessive heat my body was like a soft sponge in the fingers of a giant; perspiration oozed from me until it seemed inevitable that I should melt away at last. To open a window was a great crime, as the cotton fiber was so sensitive to wind that it would spoil. (Poor cotton fiber!) When the mill was working, the air in the mule-room was filled with a swirling, almost invisible cloud of lint, which settled on floor, machinery, and employees, as snow falls in winter. I breathed it down my nostrils ten and a half hours a day; it worked into my hair and was gulped down my throat. This lint was laden with dust, dust of every conceivable sort, and not friendly at all to lungs. . . .

A fight with a machine is the most cunning torture man can face. . . . A machine never tires, is never hungry, has no heart to make it suffer. It never sleeps, and has no ears to listen to that appeal for "mercy," which is sent to it. A machine is like Fate. It is Fate, itself. On, on, on, on it clicks, relentlessly, insistently, to the end, in the set time, in the set way! It neither goes one grain too fast or too slow. Once started, it must go on, and on, and on, to the end of the take. Such was the machine against which I wrestled—in vain. . . . The frames were ever hungry; there was always a task ahead, yes, a dozen tasks ahead, even after I had worked, exerted myself to the uttermost. I never had the consolation of knowing that I had done my work. *The machine always won.*

This author, Brown, was born in northern England in 1882. He immigrated to New Bedford, Massachusetts, with his uncle's family when he was eleven. When he was thirteen, he went to work in the mills, maintaining the dangerous machinery that spun yarn.

Lewis Hine's famous portrait of children working in a mule-room

Courtesy of Lewis Hine/National Child Labor Committee

Impoverished American and European children worked long hours, six days a week. They did not attend school and rarely had time to play with their friends. Instead they breathed the lint-filled air in cotton mills, experienced the dangers of dark coal mines, and toiled long hours doing backbreaking work in the orchards and fields.

In America it took decades for activists, such as Jane Addams, Jacob Riis, Samuel Gompers, photographer Lewis Hine, and many, many others, to change the country's attitude about working children. Through dedication and perseverance, they publicized the lives of the poor working young people. Finally a public outcry pushed the United States government to adopt strong labor laws that would protect the nation's children. Some of the workers themselves helped fuel the public outcry. Take, for instance, the "Mill Girls."

Working children posed
for this Lewis Hine
photograph

*Courtesy of Lewis
Hine/National Child
Labor Committee*

THE MILL GIRLS

Into the 1840s thousands of young women left their family farms, where their lives were isolated and difficult. Many of them went to mills in Lowell, Massachusetts, where they worked with machinery to turn cotton into cloth. Just like Gauri Maya Taming, the carpet weaver in Kathmandu, they moved far from their families. They worked under difficult conditions, thirteen hours a day. Their wages were very low. They lived six in a room in boardinghouses. One of them, Lucy Larcom (1824–1893), worked in the Lowell mills before becoming a teacher and a poet. She said, "I began to reflect upon life rather seriously for a girl of twelve or thirteen. What was I here for? What could I make of myself? Must I submit to be carried along with the current, and do just what everybody else did? No: I knew I should not do that, for there was a certain Myself who was always starting up with her own original plan or aspiration before me, and who was quite indifferent as to what people generally thought."

Although the very demanding work ravaged many lives, the once isolated farmgirls had an opportunity to meet other young women. They helped one another. They encouraged one another to learn and to read. They began to organize and fight for better conditions to ease their hard labor.

Now, more than a century later, on the other side of the world, people are organizing to fight for better conditions. As in Lowell, young people working in terrible conditions can become powerful advocates for change.

Chapter 5
"Jungle Fire"

Our first priority is to give the workers their constitutional rights. Our second priority is to educate their children.

—ESHAN ULLAH KHAN

In 1967, long before Iqbal was born, a young college student who majored in journalism was walking down one of the beautiful tree-lined streets of Lahore, an ancient city in Pakistan. He saw a nearly blind old man sitting on the sidewalk. Assuming that he needed help crossing the street, the student approached. The man was crying.

"What's wrong?" the student asked.

The old man, whose name is Baba Kullan, explained that he was a debt-bonded laborer who worked at a brickmaking kiln. He and his two daughters, ages eleven and thirteen, were sold by the owner of the kiln and his agent. The girls were raped by both the new owner and the middleman. Kullan managed to flee from the brick kiln. He said that he wanted to die.

This accidental meeting changed the life of the young journalism student. It was also a turning point for Baba Kullan, his family, and the future of debt bondage in Pakistan.

The student jumped into action. After getting a few details from the laborer, he called together a group of friends. They went to the police and demanded justice. These young men were not from landless, poor families trapped in the netherworld of bonded labor. They were middle-class college students, and the police took their request seriously. Eventually both girls were returned to their family. The news of this feat spread from worker to worker like "jungle fire."

Other laborers began to seek out the student. Their grievances were never ending. The young student soon had to choose whether to continue his studies or devote his life to helping the helpless. With the support and encouragement of his family, the student, Eshan Ullah Khan, chose the latter.

One of the first things he did was set up an organization called the Brick Kiln Workers Front. This group was a forerunner to the Bonded Labor Liberation Front (BLLF), an organization that would eventually free Iqbal.

Khan knew that his work would be dangerous. He worried about how it might affect his family. He moved out of his comfortable home and into a tiny room, one with no water and no electricity. The room also served as the new organization's office. He supported the group from his own earnings as a rookie journalist.

By the 1980s Khan's activities on behalf of the workers had landed him in prison—twelve times. He said that he spent six months in "solitary confinement in the notorious Shah Killa prison in Fort Lahore." Khan said, "To tell the story of that prison is very hard, but to struggle for human rights in Pakistan is to play with fire—I expected torture and imprisonment when I began."

In spite of the hardships, Khan has kept up a vigorous campaign against the employers and corrupt officials. Usually upbeat, he said of the employers, "They have nowhere to hide."

But they really had no reason to hide. Public apathy makes it easy for the employers to continue doing business as usual. To the manufacturers Khan was like a tiny gnat, annoying but relatively harmless, who would soon disappear.

Khan's organization did not disappear. In 1988 the Brick Kiln Workers Front extended its reach to other areas of bondage. It changed its name to the Bonded Labor Liberation Front.

It was hard for the staff to choose which abuses to work on and which ones to leave alone. There was so much to do, and they were a small

Eshan Ullah Khan, the founder and president of the Bonded Labor Liberation Front of Pakistan (BLLF), with the group's flag

*Courtesy of Ben Buxton/
Anti-Slavery International*

43

"JUNGLE FIRE"

group with very little money. Finally they agreed that they would be most effective if they concentrated all their efforts on abolishing the terrible *peshgi* system.

Later in the year a number of bonded brick kiln families were falsely arrested. Somehow one of the laborers managed to send a telegram to Pakistan's Supreme Court, describing the situation. After reviewing the case, the court ruled that the kiln workers were cruelly and illegally exploited and that the kiln owners, the police, and the district courts had conspired to take away their rights. The families were set free.

But the brick kiln owner was influential and, according to Khan's group, "held an important office in the government." No sooner had the family members left the courthouse than the police seized them again. Acting on behalf of the owner, the police beat and tortured them.

A few days later the court ruled that the bonded labor system violated the constitution of Pakistan, which guaranteed the workers rights. The Supreme Court abolished debt bondage and the *peshgi* system and granted laborers "the right to work wherever they wished."

But the Supreme Court did not go far enough. It left out an important step toward ending slavery. It did not cancel unpaid debts. This meant that the impoverished families still had to pay off their debts through the hard labor of their children. If the debt was not paid back by the time the child reached adulthood, then his children, and even perhaps his children's children, would still be responsible to the owners.

Bonded laborers all over South Asia face similar obstacles. India, for example, has the largest population on the subcontinent. It has the largest number of bonded children. It also has local human rights groups fighting on their behalf.

INDIA'S BONDED LIBERATION FRONT (BLF)

Swami Agnivesh, a Hindu monk, was a law and economics lecturer. He held an important government position. After witnessing the police shoot at a peaceful workers' demonstration, he left his position and pledged his life to helping India's laborers.

In 1981 the Swami formed the Bonded Liberation Front (BLF) of India. (Although their names and goals are similar, the BLF should not be confused with Pakistan's Bonded Labor Liberation Front, BLLF.) Three years later, in 1984, the BLF heard about thirty-two children who were kidnapped from a village in the state of Bihar. The children were compelled to weave carpets eighteen to twenty hours a day. They were branded and tortured when they made mistakes.

The BLF took up the children's case. They filed petitions in the Supreme Court of India. "The Supreme Court ordered the district administration to secure their release and appointed . . . an official Court Commissioner to investigate the conditions in small villages. . . . It resulted in the release of over 1,000 children."

Swami Agnivesh knew that release did not mean freedom. The former child slaves would never really be free unless they were given an education. According to Indian law, all children must go to school. But education is expensive. It is hard to find qualified teachers who live in the small villages and hamlets. So the BLF created Ashram Mukyi, a center for education and vocational training, to purge the newly freed children of the "slavery syndrome"—the feeling of worthlessness and the fear of "everyone they considered above them."

It quickly became clear that the local human rights groups had to find a way to raise public awareness throughout the world. To achieve that time-consuming, expensive goal they needed to join forces.

But working together in South Asia can be difficult. Since 1947, when Pakistan was partitioned from the northeast and northwest areas of India, the two countries have been adversaries. In 1971, after a bloody civil war, East Pakistan seceded from Pakistan and became Bangladesh.

Still, if the local human rights groups were ever going to put a stop to children in bondage, they had to find a way to work together.

THE SOUTH ASIAN COALITION ON CHILD SERVITUDE (SACCS)

In 1989 the secretary of India's Bonded Labor Front, Kailash Satyarthi, organized a seminar in New Delhi that brought together all the non-

government human rights organizations in the region. Also invited were international human rights observers, lawyers, judges, journalists, and twenty-two children who came from different kinds of bondage.

Two children worked in the brick kilns of Lahore. One was from the "carpet belt" in Mirzapur, India. Another came from a matchbox factory. Accompanied by local activists, each found creative ways to get to the conference. Some feigned illness or said they were visiting relatives. One boy got his older brother to cover for him at his factory.

The adults encouraged them, "Tell us about your lives as bonded laborers."

Silence.

The activists tried to be more specific. "How many hours did you work?"

Silence.

"Were you beaten?"

Silence.

The children would not say a word. They came from a world where speaking out led to punishment and beatings. Here they were together, facing tape recorders, cameras, and an assembly of impatient adults shooting questions at them.

Eventually the adults learned to slow down and give the bonded children time to adjust. Only then did the children open up. Once they felt comfortable, they had plenty to say:

> *When I started crawling my mother used to take me in the brick field where I played with the clay and also ate some of it because I was born on the brick kiln with heaps of earth around me. Later I started working with the same clay as my parents did. In this way I steadily became a* pathera [someone who works with wet clay in the brick kiln].
>
> —MANGA MASIH (NO RELATION TO IQBAL) OF FAISALABAD, PAKISTAN

> *I am 11 years old. I work in a match and fireworks factory in Vellur, Amatur. I work for 10 hours a day and get six rupees as my wage. I suffer from constant cough and eye disease. I have to work as my family is poor. I want to study in a school.*
>
> —SITA LAKSHMI OF INDIA

> *My name is Baleka. I am 10 years old. I worked in the stone quarries in Faridabad since 1984. I got no wage when I worked there for 16 hours a day. I was given a release certificate by the Collector in 1985 to Latur. I was still kept in bondage by Sharm Contractor till 1987. He sold me to Khemaji Sheth the same year. The Sheth sent me to Katejavalgo. I have not yet received anything from government. Some workers help me. I stay with my family.*
>
> —BALEKA OF FARIDABAD, INDIA

The camaraderie that emerged between the children and grown-ups brought new hope to the region's activists. Perhaps it was based on the idea that together, they could overcome bondage. They formed a new

Convention on the Rights of the Child

Children have the right to enough food, clean water, and health care.

Children have the right to an adequate standard of living.

Children have the right to be with their family or those who will care for them best.

Children have the right to protection from all exploitation and from physical, mental, and sexual abuse.

Children have the right to protection when exposed to armed conflict.

Children have the right to be protected from all forms of discrimination.

Children have the right to be protected from work that threatens their education, health, or development.

Disabled children have the right to special care and training.

Children have the right to play.

Children have the right to education.

Children have the right to have their opinions taken into account in decisions affecting their own lives.

Children have the right to know what their rights are.

alliance, the South Asian Coalition on Child Servitude (SACCS). About fifty organizations signed on, including Eshan Ullah Khan's Bonded Labor Liberation Front and Swami Agnivesh's Bonded Liberation Front.

The SACCS joined forces with large, powerful international labor and human rights organizations. Together they planned ways to teach consumers about bonded children. The group made it clear that they were not against the export of all South Asian carpets or any other goods. They were against the export of goods made by exploited children. They held press conferences with international newspapers and the media. Nightly news programs did reports about the "slave children." Bonded child labor became big news.

About the same time, in 1989, the United Nations General Assembly was working to adopt an important resolution aimed at protecting the world's children. It was called the Convention on the Rights of the Child.

In 1990 the convention was formally adopted by fifty-seven countries, including Nepal and Bangladesh. India and Pakistan signed the convention at a later date.

While all of this was going on, the self-appointed president of Pakistan, General Zia ul Haq, called for free, democratic elections. But very soon thereafter the general was killed in a mysterious plane crash. Elections went on as planned and a western-educated woman, the leader of the Pakistan People's Party, won the election. Benazir Bhutto promised to make changes. She assured her voters that she would improve worker rights and bring democracy to the people of Pakistan.

Yet bonded labor continued.

THINGS CHANGE, THINGS STAY THE SAME

Armed with new laws and access to the media, the local members of the South Asian Coalition on Child Servitude pressed their governments to monitor the factories. They demanded that the employers follow the law to determine who works in the factories. It is easier to control the activities of large factories that are in the cities. It is much more difficult to control the ones in remote towns and villages.

In rural areas carpet looms can be found in every nook and cranny, from dusty courtyards to one-room shacks.

Sixteen-year-old Laxmi has been weaving for six years. She says, "This work is good because it gives us some income. But it is very bad, too. . . . All day long we are sitting here, and it hurts our backs and legs. Little pieces of wool come into our mouths and hurt our lungs, making us sick. Our fingers are raw and give us constant pain."

Villages are still under the control of the local authorities. An invisible alliance has developed among the local carpet masters, the politi-

Former child laborers take
part in a demonstration
against child labor in
New Delhi, India,
November 8, 1996

cians, and the police. Many police officers and politicians consider bribe money to be an extension of their salaries. The scales of justice are not balanced. Indeed, when employers or agents are caught with bonded child laborers, they are not arrested. If a Pakistani bonded laborer demands justice, the police rarely bother registering an FIR (First Investigation Report), the legal report that is necessary to set the criminal justice system in motion. After several investigations, monitors from international human rights organizations said that they found "no evidence" that the police are held accountable when they do not take steps to protect bonded laborers.

Chapter 6
We Demand an End to Slavery

My parents were helpless. Our family was very poor, and low-class people are not in a position to do anything. So I personally did not ask anything of my family.

—IQBAL MASIH

At the isolated carpet factories outside villages like Muridke, there was no way for the child laborers to learn about the laws and human rights groups working on their behalf. By the time Iqbal was eight, his callused fingers were covered with tiny scars from the nicks and gashes of his sharp carpet tools. His breathing was heavy from the ever present lint particles that he ingested into his lungs.

Iqbal's father had abandoned his family years ago. Iqbal's mother remained in Muridke, working hard to provide for her children. Every once in a while Iqbal was given a day off. He spent his precious free time with his younger sister or playing soccer and cricket with friends. As a special treat he saw kung fu films that were imported from Hong Kong.

At work, when the guard was not paying careful attention, Iqbal sneaked out of the factory. One time he even went to the local police station to report the abuses that were going on at the carpet factory. Since the policeman listened and seemed genuinely concerned, Iqbal told him about the threats and the beatings and the terrible conditions. The policeman nodded in sympathy. Iqbal gave out more details. Finally the policeman said, "Come with me."

Iqbal jumped into the backseat of the policeman's car.

The policeman drove Iqbal back to the carpet factory. The guard took him into the dreaded back room, the punishment room, and gave him a terrible beating. The carpet master warned Iqbal never to try such a foolish act again. He told Iqbal that he was a working boy, a carpet weaver, and he would remain a carpet weaver for the rest of his life. There was no escape. There was no end to the work.

In spite of the threats and the beatings, Iqbal escaped from the factory many more times. He was always found and returned to the carpet master. He said that he was beaten "so many times, I could not count."

Iqbal was fined for his transgressions. His debt grew bigger and bigger. Still he ran away. When all else failed, Iqbal was chained to his loom. "I had to sit in one position for many hours. I couldn't even move during work."

When the carpet masters received larger orders for their precious export, the children were told that they had to stay at the factory and work throughout the night. Iqbal refused. He told his boss that he was in debt to work twelve hours a day and no more. As punishment for talking back and refusing to work, he was smacked on his head and his back. Nevertheless, he refused to work later than his *peshgi* required. He was taken to the punishment room, where he was tied at the knees and hung upside down. Iqbal never complained to his family because there was nothing they could do about it.

With history, tradition, and the powerful employers against him, Iqbal's options seemed few. It was most likely he would never pay back the debt because members of his family continued to borrow from the *thekedar*. The additional loans were added to Iqbal's *peshgi*. Iqbal's original 600-rupee ($12) debt grew to 13,000 rupees ($260).

In 1991 Eshan Ullah Khan's Bonded Labor Liberation Front began to gain recognition for its work against child bondage. In an attempt to educate newly freed children, it built seventy-seven schools throughout the country. These schools are called Apna Schools—Our Schools—because the bonded laborers who attended them had never

A BLLF Apna School for former bonded children from a brick kiln

Courtesy of Mats Öhman/ Bergmar Productions

had anything that they could call their own. The group also set up "Freedom Campus" to help former bonded laborers in understanding their new freedom. The schools' motto is Struggle Against Slavery Through Education. International organizations, such as UNICEF and Lidköpings U-landsförening, a Swedish organization, gave the group funding to help free more children and establish more schools.

Khan then traveled to London to ask the European Community to boycott all rugs made in Pakistan until children were no longer used as bonded laborers. He said that even his own government was operating more than a hundred centers that employed and trained children. A spokesman for the Pakistani High Commission in London denied Khan's charges, insisting that he had "never heard of such centers."

The United Nations Human Rights Commission recommended that "products such as carpets whose manufacture is liable to involve child labor should bear a special marker guaranteeing that they have not

Former child laborers
protest the exploitation
of children in India,
November 8, 1996

*Courtesy of AP Photo/
Saurabh Das*

54

been produced by children." Hundreds of newly freed children, inspired by the endorsement, demonstrated together in the streets of New Delhi, Lahore, and Kathmandu. They waved banners and shouted slogans, demanding an end to child slavery.

The following year, 1992, the Pakistani parliament passed the Bonded Labor (Abolition) Act. This law went one step further than the earlier Supreme Court ruling. It not only abolished the *peshgi* but canceled all the debts that the slave laborers' families owed to their masters. The new law included a tough penalty: a two-year minimum jail term as well as stiff fines for anyone found loaning money in return for forced labor. Perhaps now there would be a difference. Perhaps now, at long last, millions of exploited children would be free. But laws go only so far. It is up to local organizations to enforce them.

Chapter 7
Certificate of Freedom

He sat cowering in a corner, emaciated and wheezing like an old man. It was like he was trying to hide himself, to disappear, he was so frightened. But I felt there was something in this boy, that he had a strong will.
—ESHAN ULLAH KHAN

Enforcing the new law was no small task. In India bonded laborers were reported to be brutally beaten whenever they asked for the slightest increase in their salary. In other South Asian countries laborers paid a heavy price when they asked for better conditions or when they tried to organize. Any request for better treatment—a little more food or more time to go to the bathroom—was considered a "challenge" to the employer's authority. The challenge was met with severe punishment.

Eshan Ullah Khan and other BLLF members traveled from village to village, spreading the word about the new law. They held rallies and meetings in remote regions all over the country. During the rallies, they passed out a pamphlet called the *Charter of Freedom.* The pamphlet explained to the workers their rights. However, most bonded laborers are illiterate. They had to gather around someone who could read to find out what was said in the pamphlet.

The BLLF led dangerous surprise raids right into the belly of the factories. They managed to liberate hundreds of workers.

As the BLLF's activities increased, a campaign to discredit them increased as well. Employers spread nasty rumors about the BLLF.

Rural village housing in Pakistan

Courtesy of Farhad Karim

They called them a bunch of "reformers" and "abolitionists." They said that the so-called *Charter of Freedom* was Communist propaganda.

It seemed as if the BLLF was on everybody's hate list. The government called group members "Indian conspirators" because they participated in the Delhi-based South Asian Coalition on Child Servitude. They were accused of trying to destroy the economy of Pakistan by bringing down the carpet and brick industries. Factory owners hated the BLLF because they took away their cheap labor. Local authorities hated them because they exposed corruption.

Amazingly, many of the bonded laborers hated the group too. Some laborers and middlemen were suspicious: "Why would an educated man like Khan take the trouble to help the poor?"

Employers and local contractors warned the laborers to stay away from the BLLF. Anyone found talking to a BLLF volunteer would be punished. They were told not to go near that no-good, lying piece of trash—the *Charter of Freedom.* Out of fear, many laborers stayed away.

But not everyone. Freedom from bondage is too powerful a dream to be denied. More and more frequently the laborers managed to get to the rallies. More and more frequently the rallies and stories of exploited children were leaking out to the press.

"What is the alternative for these poor children?" asked a dealer who exported his carpets to the United States. "If we remove them totally, they'll starve and die, and it will be on our conscience. You have to look at it from the humanitarian point of view."

By the time Iqbal had been weaving carpets for six years, he was earning 20 rupees (40 cents) a day. In spite of the raises, his *peshgi* had grown to the point where he would never be able to buy back his bondage.

Like the other employers, Iqbal's *thekedar* warned his workers to stay away from BLLF activity. Iqbal was smart—smart enough to reason that anything the *thekedar* said was bad must be good. "My owner threatened me, but that day I ran away from work." He slipped out of the factory and attended a freedom day celebration about the rights of the bonded laborer.

It was at the freedom day celebratory rally that Iqbal first laid his eyes on the man destined to become his mentor, father figure, and best friend. Up until that moment, he had no idea that there were laws to protect child laborers, and that the *peshgi* system had been declared illegal a year earlier. He was shocked and then angry when he learned that the government had actually canceled the debt his family owed to the *thekedar.* He hovered in the corner, listening to speaker after speaker talk about justice and freedom.

During the rally, Khan noticed the tiny, shy boy crunched up in the corner. He said, "I brought him on stage and asked him to introduce himself." He told the group his name, his age, the *thekedar's* name, and the amount of his *peshgi.*

After the meeting, Iqbal refused to return to bondage. He contacted a BLLF lawyer who helped him get a freedom letter. But that was not

Former bonded carpet laborers in Pakistan

Courtesy of Mats Öhman/ Bergmar Productions

enough. Iqbal said that he could not be free unless everyone was free. He said that he had to return to the factory and tell the other boys that they could be free too.

Backed up by the BLLF, Iqbal proudly, defiantly marched up to the *thekedar* and presented his freedom letter. He called to the other boys, "Come with me and be free."

The factory owner was furious, but there was nothing he could do. Iqbal, at age ten, was finally free.

Part II
Emancipation

Chapter 8
Action

The United States must not import any products made by child labor. Period.

—United States
Senator Tom Harkin

January 1993. Thousands of miles from the stifling factories in South Asia, Tom Harkin, a United States senator from Iowa, convened a press conference. He was disturbed that the United States of America was buying goods made by the sweat of young children. He said, "It was not so long ago that we outlawed child labor in this country, and for good reason. America decided kids should spend their time in school, not in sweatshops. They realized that if businesses could not do the right thing by America's kids, then the government would have to step in and do it for them."

Senator Harkin proposed a bill called the Child Labor Deterrence Act. This bill bans the importation of any product made with child labor. It requires the United States government to keep a list of all foreign industries that use child labor. It declares that any American company importing goods from those industries would be subject to civil fines, criminal liability, or both.

Diplomats from South Asian embassies in Washington warned their countries that this challenge was real. United States inspectors and a delegation of American trade union officials paid visits to a number of garment factories in South Asia. Even before the bill was brought to a vote, manufacturers in the region began to hide their child laborers when buyers visited the factories.

Bangladeshi manufacturers were particularly anxious. They are the seventh-largest exporters of ready-made clothing to the United States. Like the other countries of South Asia, Bangladesh has laws to protect children, but no one paid much attention to them. Millions of children worked in garment factories. While many of the children were not debt bonded in the same way Iqbal had been, they worked long hours, did not go to school, and made extremely low wages. The manufacturers were clearly in violation of laws to protect children.

"The factory attendants beat me a lot," an eleven-year-old garment worker named Beauty told UNICEF. "During the buyers' visits they used to hide us inside boxes of clothes. They would say, 'If you come out here before the buyers leave, we will beat you.' Once I was practically suffocating; I thought I was going to die, so I broke the box open and came out."

Harkin's bill did not pass Congress, but he promised to reintroduce it. Foreign manufacturers wanted the senator to allow them time to figure out what to do with all the child workers. One employer said, "If the U.S. Senate allowed us, say, five years to get rid of child labor, then we could've stopped recruiting right now. This would have allowed us to keep the ones we had and enable them to become skilled under a disciplined environment."

Then Germany, a major importer of Indian carpets, proposed similar legislation. The manufacturers decided that they had better do something—fast.

South Asian manufacturers began to fire the child workers. The consequences of this were disastrous. UNICEF reported that employers fired about 50,000 children from Bangladesh's factories. In India, about 1.5 million families whose children worked in the carpet industry were faced with having no source of income. Pakistan and Nepal experienced similar problems. The freed children still had to help their families make a living. They had no skills, little or no education, and very few opportunities. They ended up with new jobs, but this was not an improvement.

> *My family was very poor and couldn't afford to send me to school. When the garment factory started, I got a job there. Without that job I'd have to work as a servant, and that's worse.*
>
> *I used to work as a domestic servant. One day I dropped a plate and it broke. The mistress of the house slapped me and shoved me out of her house. I came home crying, and my parents managed to get me a job in the garment factory. I started small. Eventually I got promoted. I became a machine operator, and my family lived on my salary. Now without that job it is hard—very, very hard. My family is suffering a lot. We can't even afford two meals a day.*
>
> —SULFA

Many children found jobs as stone crushers, street hustlers, and prostitutes. This work was much more dangerous than working long hours inside a garment factory.

The impoverished families were furious at the loss of income. "When my children cry for food, would the American government come and feed them?" a mother asked a western reporter. In time, UNICEF, the International Labor Organization (ILO), and the Bangladesh Garment Manufacturers and Export Association worked together to come up with a solution. They agreed that the child factory workers would be sent to school and that their families would receive a monthly stipend to cover some of their lost income.

That same year, 1993, a record number of nongovernmental organizations (NGOs) attended a United Nations Human Rights conference in Vienna. (Nongovernmental organizations are independent groups of activists, many of whom address and report on the human rights practices of governments all over the world. Some NGOs are large international organizations, such as Amnesty International, while others are small groups like the BLLF.) This conference provided a unique opportunity for local, grassroots groups to describe their activities before the assembled delegates, the media, and other interested parties.

Nongovernmental Organizations

Many organizations use capital letters when describing their work. For instance, nongovernmental organizations are referred to as NGOs. Here is a list of some others:

ASI: Anti-Slavery International

BLF: Bonded Liberation Front (India)

BLLF: Bonded Labor Liberation Front (Pakistan)

CMAWCL: Carpet Manufacturers Association Without Child Labor

CWIN: Child Workers in Nepal

HRCP: Human Rights Commission of Pakistan

HRW: Human Rights Watch

ILO: International Labor Organization

RMF: Rugmark Foundation

SACCS: South Asian Coalition on Child Servitude

UNHRC: United Nations Human Rights Commission

UNICEF: United Nations International Children's Emergency Fund

Doug Cahn, a representative of the Reebok Human Rights Foundation, attended the conference. He said, "The basement level of the conference hall was somewhat strangely referred to as the 'hall of horrors.' Around the room were booths, staffed by people representing NGOs from around the world. Each stall included descriptions and materials of various abuses that the group was seeking to eliminate.

"The activists took turns holding workshops or seminars throughout the day. A person could go from eight in the morning till nine at night and learn about street kids in Central America or bonded labor in Pakistan. There, at a booth, I met Eshan Ullah Khan, who was representing the Bonded Labor Liberation Front."

Children in India protesting the use of child labor in Pakistan, February 20, 1996

Courtesy of AP/John Moore

Cahn attended a seminar where Khan told the story of a recently freed bonded laborer, Iqbal Masih. "That's when I first became interested in the possibility that Iqbal himself might someday be a worthy applicant for the Reebok Human Rights Award," said Cahn. "Iqbal was not someone we had heard of before, and it seemed to us that the issue of child bondage was not well understood in the United States."

That chance meeting in the "hall of horrors" would later have a profound effect on Doug Cahn, on the rest of the staff at the Reebok Foundation, and most of all on Iqbal Masih himself.

Chapter 9
A Proper Schoolboy . . . and Activist

Iqbal and I had a long conversation, and he was great. He was very articulate. He was remarkable. And very sweet. He didn't have a serious demeanor. He was smarter and more articulate than most kids I know, but ultimately he was a kid. He'd make a great organizer.

—FARHAD KARIM, FORMER
RESEARCHER, HUMAN RIGHTS
WATCH/ASIA

Eshan Ullah Khan arranged for Iqbal to move to Lahore and study at BLLF's Freedom Campus. The distance from Muridke, Iqbal's home, to Lahore is about eighteen miles. To a young person like Iqbal, it might as well have been 18,000 miles. Once again the boy's young life changed. He now lived in a beautiful, ancient city, the cultural center of Pakistan.

The busy streets, packed buses, and people from all levels of society are very different from Iqbal's sleepy, dusty village. Street merchants sell everything imaginable: food, clothing, flowers, toys. Children are everywhere. Working young people, like Iqbal once had been, sell fruit from sidewalk stalls, pump gas, and run errands. Schoolchildren, like Iqbal had now become, play cricket in the park and take school trips to the old fort, the ancient palaces, and the marble mosques. Best of all, Lahore has movie theaters, where Iqbal could watch kung fu movies and cartoons during his free time. Free time! Imagine that!

From every account, Iqbal studied hard, learning to read and write in Urdu. He was so smart and so eager to learn that he completed five semesters of work in only two years. He was a natural leader who instinctively looked after his school chums. If a classmate did not show up for classes, he would go to his home to find out why. Was he ill? Did she need a copy of the classwork?

He returned home often to visit with his family. He played with his little sister and taught her the alphabet and numbers. Iqbal's sister was madly in love with her big brother—her student-brother. His mother, Inayat Bibi, was proud of the fact that her son was the first person in their entire family to get an education.

Once Iqbal learned to read and write, his horizons grew broader. He must have studied about slavery in America because he said, "I want to be like Abraham Lincoln and free the slave children of Pakistan."

Iqbal joined other BLLF volunteers and roamed the countryside. He took part in demonstrations, proudly waving a BLLF flag, shouting to all who could hear, "We are free!" He visited carpet factories and brought his message of freedom to the children working there. "You should come with me and be free," he told them. And like Lincoln, or perhaps a modern Pied Piper, Iqbal led thousands of children to freedom.

BLLF schoolgirls

Courtesy of Mark Shapiro

Iqbal at a demonstration
with other formerly
bonded children

*Courtesy of Britt-Marie
Klang/Bergmar Productions*

Journalists, labor leaders, and human rights activists from around the world visited the Freedom Campus. They met with Iqbal, who represented the school as the president of the children's wing.

The young student, smartly dressed in a blue school uniform, spoke in front of many groups. He was strong. He was passionate. People, children especially, listened. He told the audience about his life as a carpet weaver. He talked about other boys who spent long hours in front of the looms. He talked about the abuses, the beatings, the starvation. Mostly he talked about the injustice of robbing poor children of their childhood. He was amazingly articulate, considering the fact that he was barely literate and had no life experiences other than bondage.

In Iqbal, Khan found an extraordinary speaker who could go on for hours without looking at notes, without missing an issue. Adults could talk until they were blue in the face about the exploitation of children. To hear it from the mouth of a child who experienced the horror was much more powerful. He was not one bit intimidated by the large crowds who came to hear him. In fact, he enjoyed them.

About this time, a new smear campaign appeared. It began with a few threatening letters addressed to Iqbal. Then, according to Khan, there were some death threats. Iqbal paid no attention to them. He could not imagine that an adult would actually harm him. Boldly he told his friends that the threats encouraged him to work harder.

RUGMARK

The South Asian Coalition on Child Servitude had been meeting with several major manufacturers and exporters to try to settle their differences. The group also sent representatives to Geneva to ask the United Nations Human Rights Commission to adopt a labeling system to inform the public about which products were not made by children. In 1991 the commission put out a report. It recommended

> that products such as carpets whose manufacture is liable to involve child labor should bear a special mark guaranteeing that they have not been produced by children. In this context consumers should be alerted so that they will demand products bearing such a mark.

About fifty carpet manufacturers pledged never to use child labor in their units. The SACCS immediately set up an independent agency that included nongovernmental groups involved in the issue, carpet manufacturers, importers, exporters, and international organizations such as UNICEF. The agency was given the authority to label carpets that were made without child labor. A German export promotion group took the responsibility of setting up the system for inspections and labeling. On September 5, 1994, after years of meetings and debates, the Rugmark Foundation was formally established. Its label is a smiling carpet logo.

Each label has a computerized code number that identifies the exporter, manufacturer, loom owner, and weaver. All the carpet manufacturers and exporters can apply for this label so long as they agree to produce carpets free of child labor. To check that the manufacturer is living up to the agreement, agents make unannounced, random inspections to all the factories.

Some manufacturers would not join the foundation. They said that the system would never work, that it would be impossible to patrol so many carpet centers. But many others came on board.

Once the foundation was in place, the attention focused on how to help the freed children. Even though the partners of Rugmark believe that primary responsibility for the children's education and rehabilitation belongs to the government, they set up a fund to educate and rehabilitate the freed carpet children. This fund is paid for from a small portion of the sale of adult-made carpets. At last consumers had a certified guarantee that carpets are manufactured without child labor.

By this time Khan had become a father figure to Iqbal. In November 1994 he took Iqbal to the International Labor Organization's conference in Stockholm. Iqbal eloquently described his life as a debt-bonded worker. During his free time, he visited Swedish schools and met young people his own age.

Rugmark symbol

Meanwhile, the staff at the Reebok Foundation continued to keep
tabs on the amazing accomplishments of young Iqbal. Communications
with Pakistan were not easy. It was difficult to get reliable information
about the BLLF and Iqbal. Journalists and human rights activists who
had visited BLLF schools described the classes and wrote recommen-
dations for Iqbal. The foundation staff decided that the time had come
to honor Iqbal Masih with a Reebok Human Rights Award.

The award was established to pay tribute to young women and men
less than thirty years old who make significant contributions to the
fight for human rights. It usually takes years of activism to accomplish
this. Iqbal was so much younger than any of the prior honorees that the
foundation decided to create a new category for younger activists who
are working to make a difference. Iqbal Masih became the recipient of
the Reebok Youth in Action Award. He and Eshan Ullah Khan were
invited to Boston to participate in the gala award presentation.

Because of Iqbal's age and his inexperience, the staff at Reebok
suggested that he come to Boston a week earlier than the other award

winners. They thought he would need a little extra time to adjust to America. There would be meetings with international award winners, civic leaders, rock stars, movie stars, and politicians. He would be speaking before a large audience. He would be participating in many interviews, complete with cameras rolling and lights glaring. Would the former child slave be able to handle it?

Chapter 10
Just Like Abraham Lincoln

*When Iqbal spoke to us, he made me look at what I had differently. He
showed me that it was wrong to take things for granted and that it was
important to speak out against things that were wrong. I thought, if
Iqbal could make a difference, so could I.*

—Amanda Loos, a fourteen-
year-old student at Broad
Meadows Middle School,
Quincy, Massachusetts

Iqbal strode off the plane, smartly dressed in his white *shalwaar kamiz,*
baggy trousers with a long shirt over it, a wool sweater, and a winter
jacket to protect him from Boston's cold December air. A British Airways flight bag was slung over his shoulder. He and Eshan Ullah Khan
were met at the airport by Sharon Cohen, the vice president of
Reebok's public affairs division, and her friend Leonard Fein.

Sharon said to Iqbal, "I've read so much about you, I don't know
whether to speak to you as a child or as a man."

"I am a child," he told her.

Sharon drove Iqbal and Eshan Ullah Khan to a lodging in Cambridge,
a block and a half from her home. For the next ten days Iqbal spent much
of his free time in the home that Sharon shares with Sarah, her daughter.

Paula Van Gelder, a foundation staff member, spent time with Iqbal
too. She said, "The first day we just got to know him. Mr. Khan acted
as the translator. It was very low-key." The Reebok staff was shocked
at Iqbal's size. He looked so tiny, like a six-year-old. But his eyes were
bright and his skin was clear, except for a scar over his right eyebrow
where he had been hit with a carpet tool. They could not help but
notice that his hands, working hands, were covered with tiny scars.

The staff presented Iqbal with Reebok sneakers as a "welcome to America" present. Iqbal said that he liked Boston; there were so many Christmas trees. He liked the twinkling lights on the trees and the ones that lined the tall buildings. He liked the fact that he could watch cartoons, especially ones with animals in them, right in his very own room.

Iqbal's days were filled with sight-seeing, school visits, and interviews. He saw *The Lion King* and an IMAX movie about the jungle. Always proud of his heritage, he told the Americans, "Yes, I liked the movies very much, but we have movies in Pakistan, too."

He was fascinated with Walk/Don't Walk signals at street intersections. That they did not have in Pakistan. He quickly learned a few English words: *Christmas trees, walk/don't walk, hello, thank you, free.*

He visited big department stores—stores that sell carpets made in South Asia. The carpets, possibly made by bonded children (there were no Rugmark labels), were sold at prices that seemed very high to the former four-dollar-a-week worker. Iqbal was totally shocked.

For his second day in Boston, the foundation organizers arranged a visit to the Friends' School in Cambridge. Eshan Ullah Khan was away, meeting with American human rights organizations. Since Iqbal did not speak English, Reebok provided a translator.

Iqbal's visit caused a sensation at the school. With the help of the translator, Iqbal spent time with the students, playing computer games and comparing their lives. The one reporter who was present was told not to ask questions. This was just a chance for Iqbal to get to know American children. Reebok did not want Iqbal to feel that he was on display.

That night Iqbal, Khan, and about ten people from the foundation, as well as their children, had dinner at an Italian restaurant that was known for great pizza. Iqbal hated the pizza. The chef made him risotto. It tasted like the rice he ate back home. He loved it. Paula's nephew, who was about the same age as Iqbal, brought along his computer game, Game Boy. They played it throughout the meal.

In his spare time Iqbal watched as many cartoons as possible. He was especially intrigued about a certain rabbit with very long ears who got in and out of all kinds of trouble. He told the grown-ups, in minute detail, about each escapade. Once again Khan acted as the translator, patiently, faithfully—even when it became boring—translating every word.

Sharon took Iqbal for a complete checkup at Boston's famed Children's Hospital. They sat together for hours, waiting for tests and X rays. Sharon said, "He was adorable and brave and a very good patient. He was an upbeat child, always smiling and agreeable."

The doctors who examined him said that even though Iqbal was undersize, he had not yet reached puberty. They diagnosed him as having "psychosocial dwarfism"—his small stature was caused by environmental rather than genetic factors. Malnutrition and years spent hunched over a carpet loom in an unventilated room had stunted his growth, curved his spine, and weakened his lungs. He had problems with his kidneys. In fact, the Reebok staff had to make certain that Iqbal knew exactly where the bathroom was wherever he went. Sharon remembers the funny way he told people that he was going to the bathroom. He would say, "I'm going to the department."

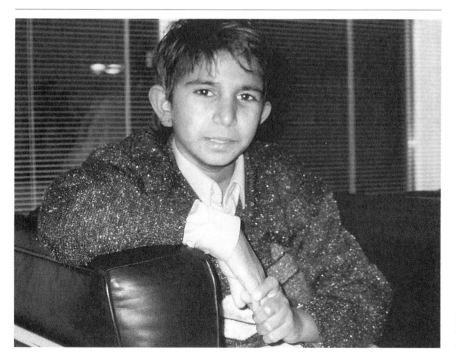

Iqbal in Boston

Courtesy of Sharon Cohen

Miraculously, the X rays showed that Iqbal's growth plates were open, so he could still grow. The doctors thought that growth hormones might work. (Later a Swedish friend arranged for a Swedish drug company to donate a year's worth of expensive hormone medicine.)

After a long day with the doctors, Sharon took Iqbal to F.A.O. Schwarz. He went right to the computer games.

At night he visited Sharon and her daughter. He would spin around and around on Sharon's swivel chair. Then he would dive into Sharon's lap, wrap his arms and legs around her, and cuddle. Iqbal was a great cuddler.

At one point he said to Sharon: "You—mama, me—son." Three-year-old Sarah was like a baby sister to him. He constantly patted her on the head in a brotherly fashion.

When the three of them went outside, Iqbal reached up and held Sharon's hand as they crossed the street. Finally Sarah asked her mother, "When is Iqbal going home?" She was used to having her mother to herself, and this new brother was getting too much attention.

Iqbal and Sarah Cohen

Courtesy of Sharon Cohen

The following day Iqbal visited Broad Meadows Middle School, a low-income public school in Quincy, Massachusetts, a suburb of Boston. When Iqbal arrived, the students were studying the origins of the Civil War and the roots of the industrial revolution in the United States. They learned how the country developed from farming to factories. They had already read Charles Dickens's *Oliver Twist*, the novel that had educated the English about the horrors of child labor. Now they were about to meet a modern Oliver who was trying to educate the world about the current version of child labor.

In preparing for the visit, teacher Ron Adams gave his class all kinds of projects. Students checked the carpet in the main hall of the school to see if it was made by bonded laborers. They breathed a sigh of relief when they saw that it was machine-made in Belgium. Some students telephoned carpet stores and asked if they sold rugs with the Rugmark label. One student wrote to Senator Edward Kennedy and asked about his stand on child labor.

Iqbal arrived at the school with Sharon, Paula, an interpreter, a reporter, and a photographer from *The Christian Science Monitor*. He was met at the door by a student named Kevin Piccuito. "My job was to welcome Iqbal into the building. I escorted him to the classroom and introduced him to the class. When he was telling his story, I could not believe that he was still alive after all the beatings he got from the factory owners."

Iqbal walked into the classroom and said, "I understand that you are studying slavery in the United States. I'm here to tell you it is still alive." He astonished the students by his descriptions of a life in slavery.

"Were you beaten?" asked Dan Long.

"I couldn't even count how many times."

Iqbal told the class that his *thekedar* told the workers that it was the Americans who ordered the Pakistanis to make carpets. For so many years Iqbal wondered, Who are these Americans who make children suffer so much just for a rug? He said he was happy to finally see that Americans are not demons with horns. Dan said, "I was glad to see him smile."

The American students asked lots of questions, and he answered every one of them. The translator was exhausted. Iqbal was exhilarated. Once again the reporter was invited to listen in, but only the young people asked questions.

"Didn't you miss your mother?"

"Well, I saw my mother. I would see her every night."

"Were you mad at your father for doing that?"

"Well, I wasn't happy, but I knew why."

"How did you feel when you couldn't play?"

Iqbal explained that he didn't know then that was what other children got to do.

One student asked if he feared for his life.

"I don't think about it," Iqbal replied.

Iqbal's talk left the students breathless. The lessons of the past had been ignored. Pakistan was a developing country, just like the United States had been more than a hundred years ago. Developing countries were making the same mistakes the United States and England made.

Iqbal was in for a few surprises, too. Student Amy Papile told him, "I've written a letter to Mrs. Bhutto [the prime minister of Pakistan] and I told her that she should listen to the children when they speak. And because she's a woman and because people don't always listen to women, she should understand what it is like not to be heard." Another student, Robert Dilks, said, "Yesterday my mother was going to buy a rug. I asked her if it was made in Pakistan with child bonded labor. She said, 'With what?' I said, 'There is someone coming to our class from Pakistan who was sold at age four to a carpet factory as a bonded slave laborer.' She was surprised. I was surprised."

Iqbal was astonished!

Student Jen Grogan said that later in the lunchroom "nobody was eating. Everybody was up around the table where he sat. Some people were standing on tables because they couldn't see him."

At the end of the day the students gave Iqbal presents: a backpack, a school shirt, an honorary membership at the school, a Hacky Sack, a 1976 bicentennial medal, a book about the mills in Lowell, Massachusetts. Jen said that she gave Iqbal "a note, a picture, a friendship bracelet, three gum balls, instant hot cocoa, and some white rice."

One girl gave him a kiss. He asked Paula, "Who was that girl in the

Iqbal Masih in the cafe-
teria of the Broad
Meadows Middle School,
surrounded by his new
friends, December 2, 1994

Courtesy of Ron Adams

red dress?" Another student made a painting of him. Someone else
wrote a song in his honor.

When Iqbal was about to leave, the teacher let the class go to say
good-bye. Before departing, Iqbal got out of the car to shake hands and
say good-bye. The class promised to join Iqbal in the fight to free the
bonded children. This was a day that no one would ever forget.

Khan, ever watchful that all the attention would go to Iqbal's head,
said, "You have to share all this with the other children back home
because they don't have this."

"Yep!" he replied.

"You have to go back and study."

"Yep!"

By the end of the week, the other Reebok Human Rights Award
winners began arriving from countries around the globe. Iqbal and
Khan moved to the hotel where all the award winners would be
lodged. Khan watched cartoons with Iqbal just to keep him company

Iqbal with teacher
Ron Adams at the Broad
Meadows Middle School

Courtesy of Ron Adams

and give him a break between the constant interviews he had to give. There were newspaper reporters, radio show hosts, and television newscasters all wanting to meet the young former slave. Iqbal gladly answered their questions.

That night about twenty award winners met in the hotel lobby to have a meal together at an Indian restaurant. As they walked to the restaurant, Iqbal appointed himself the leader of the group. At every intersection, he told the older winners when they could cross and when they could not. Then he would take Sharon's hand before crossing the street.

The foundation hosts were aware that Iqbal never wore the new Reebok sneakers they had given him as a welcoming present. Paula asked him if the shoes did not fit. "No," he said, pointing to his clothing. "Shirt—Pakistan, pants—Pakistan, shoes—Pakistan."

The Americans could not help but notice how organized Iqbal was. He carried his British Airways flight bag everywhere. Everything was neat and in order. His hotel key was in one pocket and his pens were in another. He would open his vest and there was a little pocket where eight pens were all lined up, rather like a street merchant who flips open his jacket to reveal lines of watches for sale. He carried the pens along with his carpet tools as props when he spoke. He would hold up a pen and say, "This is the tool that children should have." And then he would hold up his carpet tool and say, "This is the tool of the bonded laborer."

Two nights before the big award ceremony, more winners arrived at the hotel. The dinner group grew to forty people. They went to a private room at the Italian restaurant where Iqbal had had his first, and only, taste of pizza. After dinner the award winner from Haiti spontaneously started singing. And then another winner sang. Iqbal stood up and sang his school song. Finally the winner from Northern Ireland recited poetry.

The night before the award ceremony, there was a fancy-dress dinner. Iqbal arrived, splendid in his white *shalwaar kamiz,* a red vest, and for the first time wearing the new Reebok sneakers. He went from table to table meeting the guests and saying hello to his new friends. A harpist played throughout the meal. The harp fascinated Iqbal. At the end of each set, he would go up and inspect the beautiful instrument.

When Sharon Cohen was about to give a speech about the Reebok award winners, she asked the person who was sitting next to Iqbal to make sure that he stood up at the end. But when Iqbal heard his name mentioned, he got up, walked to the front of the room, and stood beside Sharon. She finished her speech with Iqbal right next to her.

The president of Brandeis University, Jehuda Reinharz, was in the audience. Leonard Fein suggested that he give Iqbal a scholarship to Brandeis. Without missing a beat, Reinharz said, "Yes." He announced that when Iqbal turned eighteen, if he qualified, he would be happy to grant him a university scholarship. Iqbal was thrilled that one day he could go to college. He marched over to the president and hugged him.

The morning of the ceremony finally arrived. People gathered backstage at Northeastern University's auditorium. A security guard found Paula and delivered a package from two Broad Meadows Middle School students. Inspired by Iqbal's visit, they had canvassed the neighborhood and got people to write 656 letters protesting child bondage. The letters were going to be sent to Prime Minister Benazir Bhutto, President Clinton, Senators Edward Kennedy and John Kerry, state representatives, the United Nations, and forty-five local carpet stores. But first they wanted Iqbal to see them. Iqbal was absolutely thrilled. He was making a difference. And his friends at Broad Meadows Middle School were coming through for him. Together they would fight to end child bondage.

Iqbal stepped up to the stage, and actor Blair Underwood introduced him:

> Three thousand years ago, in a call that has echoed through the centuries and the millennia, a man named Moses thundered, "Let my people go." But Pharaoh would not let them go, so they fled, and as he chased them, they crossed the Red Sea from slavery into freedom, laying down a path that other peoples throughout history have followed. In our own country, we fought a bloody civil war before crossing our Red Sea, and still today we see the scars that slavery inflicts. . . .

Iqbal with harpist

Courtesy of Richard Sobel/ Reebok Human Rights Foundation

*Courtesy of Richard Sobel/
Reebok Human Rights
Foundation*

He closed his introduction with the pronouncement: *"Iqbal Masih,
leader, inspiration, giant: we honor you with the Reebok Youth in Action
Award."*

Iqbal proudly, confidently gave his speech.

The day after the awards, a reporter from ABC News interviewed
Iqbal for their Friday segment "Person of the Week."

While Iqbal and the ABC reporter walked around Cambridge, Khan
was talking business with Reebok. The award ceremony came with a
monetary award, $10,000 for Iqbal's education and $15,000 to the
BLLF to help run their programs.

Khan did not want to control Iqbal's money. He asked, "Please keep
the money for Iqbal here in the United States. If you can, invest it for
him and keep it separate." At the time, the foundation did not understand why Khan was so insistent on this. It wasn't until much later,
when Khan was accused by critics of stealing money from Iqbal, that
they understood the activist's reasoning.

Finally it was time to go home to Pakistan. A big white limo pulled up to the hotel to carry Iqbal and Khan to the airport. The foundation staff along with the hotel personnel all came out to say good-bye. Paula said, "The last thing I remember was Iqbal in the backseat of the limo, his head turned to us, as he drove away."

Chapter 11
Return to Pakistan

Iqbal Masih was very affectionate to my family. Whenever he came to this area, he made it a point to visit us.

—AMANAT MASIH, IQBAL'S
MATERNAL UNCLE

Iqbal returned, triumphant, to Freedom Campus in Lahore. He told his classmates about his exciting adventure in the States—the people he met, the places he had visited. As promised, he shared his many gifts with them. Then he settled down to his studies and to the task of liberating more bonded children from factories. His travels and international acclaim gave him even greater self-confidence than before. He bragged to his friends how he turned the tables on his boss. "I'm not afraid of the owner any longer. Now he's afraid of me."

The death threats increased. Iqbal refused to stop liberating the other children. His campaign led to the closure of dozens of carpet-weaving factories in his district. Khan said, "He was so brave. . . . You can't imagine. He managed to free thousands of children."

The president of the Islamabad Carpet Exporters Association told his colleagues, "Our industry is the victim of enemy agents who spread lies and fictions around the world that bonded labor and child labor is utilized in the production of hand-knotted carpets. They are not and have never been." He condemned the BLLF and its allies as "Jewish and Indian enemies who want to damage the reputation of Pakistan's carpet industry."

I. A. Rehman, the director of the Human Rights Commission of Pakistan, responded to the absurd claim: "These charges flew in the face not just of reason but also of an extraordinary amount of evidence. Anywhere else they would have been laughed at and dismissed. Here they were accepted as fact and acted on."

April 16, 1995. Iqbal went home to Muridke to visit his family for the Easter holiday. "He had come to see us on Easter. In the evening, he had left to see his uncle, Amanat," Inayat Bibi later explained. "He said that he had urgent work in Lahore and he must reach there the same day. I tried to stop him from going to Lahore, but he said, 'Mother, I have to take my medicine daily without fail. There should be no break.'

"Eshan Ullah Khan was administering him some potion for improvement in his height." This must have been the growth hormone that had been donated by the Swedish drug company. (Iqbal's friends at Reebok had recently learned that the hormone treatments had showed early signs of success.)

Amanat Masih, Iqbal's maternal uncle, was an illiterate farmworker. He tilled eight acres of land that he rented from a nearby factory owner. He and his wife had nine children, three sons and six daughters.

At about seven in the evening, Iqbal arrived at his uncle's house. Amanat said, "I was away watering my fields. Two other landworkers were there also. One was a man by the name of Ashraf. The other man's name was Yousaf Khwara. Their lands are adjacent [to mine], and they were also watering their fields." At one point Ashraf told Amanat that he was feeling "giddy," and he went home to have a cup of tea.

Iqbal, his cousin Liaqat (Amanat's son), and his friend Faryad hopped on a bicycle to bring Amanat his evening meal. Amanat said, "It was their daily routine. Iqbal met them coming to the fields to bring me my meal and, keen to see me before returning to Lahore, had joined them. Faryad was pedaling, Liaqat sat on the carrier at the back, and Iqbal sat sideways on the front rod." The dirt road was a deserted, plainlike stretch of land that linked a *ketcha* (an unpaved or raw) road to the fields. The place was desolate that evening, no traffic at all.

Iqbal sat on the crossbar of the bike, a way people often ride in Pakistan. Suddenly they came upon Ashraf.

Shots rang out. Faryad was hit in the arm, but Iqbal was struck in the back and side. He died instantly.

"I heard the sound of gunfire and then shrieks of my son Liaqat and of Faryad. They were calling out to me for help," Amanat reported. "When Yousaf and I rushed there, Iqbal Masih was on the ground, bleeding. My donkey cart, which my neighbor Shada had borrowed to carry fodder, stood close by. Faryad had pellet injuries on his left arm, while Liaqat was unhurt.

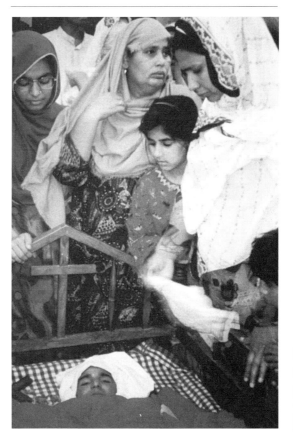

Inayat Bibi and her
daughter at Iqbal's
funeral

Courtesy of
John Van Hasselt/Sygma

"We left the children with Iqbal's dead body and rushed to inform Ashraf's employers, Zaki and Ali Hussain, about what he had done. Zaki and Ali and the two of us then set off to look for Ashraf. We first went to the village where he lived. We found Ali's gun there, but there was no trace of Ashraf. Then we went to Ferozewala police station to register an FIR [First Investigation Report]. This was done on the report of Faryad, who was an eyewitness to the incident. The police meanwhile went out to examine the place of occurrence for themselves."

Iqbal's mother learned of her son's death at about nine or ten that evening. She sat among her friends, mourning her loss. She said, "His height was very short for his age, but he talked like a grown-up. He was destined to be a big man."

Iqbal was buried the following day at the edge of the Christian grave-yard near the Masihs' home. In spite of the short notice, eight hundred mourners, including international journalists, attended the funeral. Iqbal was proclaimed a "martyr for the cause of bonded labor."

Young activists at a labor
demonstration in Lahore

Courtesy of
John Van Hasselt/Sygma

After the funeral, Iqbal's family returned to the road where the killing
had occurred. They placed a brick where Iqbal died as a reminder of
his life and as a symbol of their loss.

Later, more than three thousand protesters, mostly young children,
marched through the streets of Lahore. In honor of Iqbal's memory,
they demanded an end to child labor.

Prime Minister Benazir Bhutto called the killing an "outrage" and
ordered a special payment for Iqbal's family. (It was never paid.) She
vowed to fight child labor. (Her government continued to take only lim-
ited action.)

At the opening session of a meeting of the Working Group at the
United Nations Human Rights Commission, they observed a moment
of silence in honor of Iqbal and "all victims of contemporary forms of
slavery, especially children."

Eshan Ullah Khan called a press conference. He said, "It was very
clear he had only one enemy—the carpet mafia." Four days after
Iqbal's death, Khan flew to Europe to consult with other activists and

to call upon the United Nations Human Rights Commission to ban the import and sale of all products made by children, especially carpets. "I appeal to importers and consumers: say no and only no to child-made carpets. This is the last message of Iqbal. It would be an insult to his blood and memory if people continue to buy child-made products in any part of the world."

The police investigation report disagreed with Khan's conclusion: "Iqbal Masih did not have enemies. He did not become a target of the carpet mafia."

A small landowner and his laborer were arrested. The government's finding was that the murder was a random act of violence.

Chapter 12
Who Killed Iqbal Masih?

I had never met Iqbal before. I fired in utter confusion. I am an absolutely impoverished man. I am not familiar with rich persons. I have no acquaintance with any carpet manufacturer. I am supported by my parents through hard labor. [My bosses] are simple people and have no business except tilling the land. They have nothing to do with the carpet business. I have given the same statement to the police.

—ASHRAF, AKA HERO

Ashraf, also known as Hero, was a laborer who worked the land next to Iqbal's uncle's. His was a very poor family. His father was blind, and his brother was a street vendor. Besides farming, he also knew how to drive a tractor, although he did not have a driver's license.

On the night of Iqbal's murder, Ashraf left the field and went to a nearby *dera* (meeting place). Amanat's neighbor, Shada, asked Ashraf to do him a favor and return a donkey cart that he had borrowed from Iqbal's uncle. A gun belonging to Ashraf's employer had been left at the *dera*. He took it along with him.

Ashraf drove the donkey cart down the deserted dirt road. High on *bhang*, an intoxicant, he stopped the cart, got out, and began abusing the donkey. Just at that time, the three boys were biking down the road. Liaqat recognized his father's donkey and cart. Then, according to Ashraf's confession, "The three boys, all riding the bike, started a hue and cry. I picked up the gun and fired. Iqbal Masih got hit."

At the time he said that he didn't know Iqbal. "When Iqbal Masih fell, I ran to the *dera* with the gun. I stayed there for about an hour and a half, then left the gun there and escaped."

Ashraf's employer was arrested because the gun that killed Iqbal belonged to him. He was later released.

This description of Iqbal's murder was taken from an independent investigation by the Human Rights Commission of Pakistan. As the months passed, the participants changed their stories over and over again.

THE INVESTIGATION

The staff at the Reebok Human Rights Foundation tried to follow the fast-changing events surrounding Iqbal's murder. Paula Van Gelder said, "There were so many twists and turns, and we were trying hard to keep up. Someone from the BLLF in Pakistan sent information to Sweden. They in turn sent it to us." The Reebok Foundation and other international human rights groups called for a full, independent investigation into Iqbal's death. Before Iqbal was buried, an autopsy was performed. The report included some oral accounts of the killing and a diagram of Iqbal's body, showing where the wounds were. This was not nearly enough data to determine how and why Iqbal was killed. At Reebok's request, a forensic specialist from Physicians for Human Rights evaluated the autopsy report. "The autopsy report and police report," the specialist concluded, "leave many questions unanswered." More than fifty governments and human rights groups condemned the police investigation.

Not trusting the local officials, the independent, nongovernmental organization Human Rights Commission of Pakistan (HRCP) did its own investigation. It interviewed Ashraf, the confessed killer, and members of Iqbal's family. Everyone, including Iqbal's mother, told the commission that the carpet industry had nothing to do with Iqbal's tragic death. The relationship between the Human Rights Commission of Pakistan and the Bonded Labor Liberation Front was not friendly, however, and the BLLF would not allow the two eyewitnesses who had recently moved to BLLF headquarters to speak to the commission.

After reviewing the interviews, the Human Rights Commission of Pakistan concluded that Ashraf had acted alone. The carpet manufacturers played no role in the murder. This conclusion deepened the rift between the Human Rights Commission of Pakistan and the BLLF, which still believed the death was caused by the carpet manufacturers.

Since the HRCP report Ashraf has retracted his confession. Iqbal's mother moved to the BLLF offices in Lahore. She has changed her opinion about her son's death as well. Some antislavery crusaders continue to believe that the chance-death story was made up to protect the carpet industry.

FALLOUT

After Eshan Ullah Khan's public allegations, western countries began canceling millions of dollars of carpet orders. Children all over the world rallied to Iqbal's cause. When Prime Minister Bhutto visited Stockholm, Swedish schoolchildren protested against child labor in Pakistan in front of the Pakistani embassy. One Pakistani official said, "Never before have we had so many people demanding certificates that exports were not manufactured by children working as laborers."

Some carpet manufacturers, concerned about the tremendous loss of revenue, counterattacked. They said that Eshan Ullah Khan and the BLLF were trying to exploit the tragedy by involving them in the murder.

They said that Khan had taken Iqbal's money. They called on the government to take "appropriate" action against the BLLF for "harming the national interest with false propaganda."

Khan, still in Europe, was charged with sedition and mounting economic warfare against Pakistan. These charges carry the death penalty.

The police raided BLLF offices. Their files and equipment were confiscated. Two people were arrested, a volunteer and an accountant. No one was allowed to talk to them, not even their lawyer. They were not freed until Amnesty International stepped in and protested their arrests.

Local papers assured their readers that carpet workers live better than the average citizen. "The few children working on carpets do so after school, in their own homes, under the supervision of loving parents."

CHANGING TIMES . . .

On December 10, 1996, the Supreme Court of India mandated the creation of a trust fund to be established by the government and the employers that break the child labor laws. This fund will help provide compulsory education for working children. It further urged a program to provide jobs to adult family members instead of their children.

Less than a year later, on October 10, 1997, the president of the United States, Bill Clinton, signed into law a ban on imported goods made by bonded child laborers.

Along with Rugmark, six new labeling programs are now in operation. In addition, a number of transnational carpet companies hire their own inspectors to monitor the family and factory looms that make their carpets. However, questions continue to be raised about whether these inspection and labeling programs are beyond the influence of corruption.

To this day, new allegations and explanations about Iqbal's death are described in articles, in films, and on the Internet. Will we ever know the truth? Or, as in President Kennedy's assassination, will the facts forever be surrounded in controversy?

For now, Iqbal's murder remains a mystery. Children being forced into bonded labor remains a fact.

Part III
Reconstruction

Chapter 13
A School for Iqbal

Well, that day I got a phone call from my father, and he said that some kid at our school had died, and I was, like, who? And he said, "I don't know exactly, but his name was Iqbal Masih." And I was, like, oh no, not him. So I called my friend, and he felt sad. I felt sad too. I left the house and walked to the beach and skipped rocks, and I felt a tear come on and I tried to hold it in but couldn't. So at school I expressed my feelings in letters and drawings to help the investigation of his death and to build a school for Pakistani children.

—DIDIER ALTHER, A THIRTEEN-YEAR-OLD BROAD MEADOWS STUDENT

Iqbal's death came just four and a half months after his visit to Broad Meadows Middle School, in Quincy, Massachusetts. The students were on spring break. When a Sunday night news program reported that Iqbal Masih had been shot and killed, there was disbelief and shock. Students began calling one another. "Did you hear? . . . It can't be. . . . Who would shoot a child? . . . Could it be that he was shot for speaking out?"

The following day many students converged on the school. Ron Adams, the teacher who had invited Iqbal to meet with his class, was also the track coach. He held practice every day, even during spring break. He canceled track practice and opened a classroom for the mourning students. He said, "They were angry. They were furious. Iqbal's murder had a profound effect on these young people. Even though they had only met him once, for one day, Iqbal had become a symbol to them. His voice and his message had touched them deeply. They were determined that they were not going to let a bullet silence Iqbal's message: that all children should be free and in school."

The students formed a circle and held a moment of silence, where they in their own way said a little prayer for Iqbal, for his family, and for other children like Iqbal. They were numb. Amanda Loos said that she was "shocked and devastated." And that's the way the teacher felt too. He asked himself, Is it really true that if you are a kid and you speak out, you will be silenced? Is this really the way the world is?

Adams knew that he had to find a way to channel the anger into something positive. "The best thing to do was to vent. They unloaded a lot of anger at the meeting but still left unanswered the question: What are we going to do about this?"

Karen Marin, a student, said, "We promised Iqbal we were going to fight to the end and get those kids free. Even though Iqbal's not there to help us . . . we've got to try something really big now 'cause he's gone."

The first thing they did was circulate a petition asking for an independent investigation into Iqbal's murder. "Let's work for justice. Let's catch whoever did this." At the town square, they were amazed that people walking down the street, adults, stopped and listened to them. Strangers signed the petition, and some even tried to donate money. The students did not want money; that was not what they were looking for. But the pedestrians said, "I think you will do more than circulate a petition, so here's money for your next step."

The students were very pleased with the response. Many of the adults had never heard of Iqbal. This was one way to keep his memory alive.

The following week school was back in session. The students met to discuss what to do with the petition. Adams said, "We decided to mail it to Amnesty International because we thought that they would know how to get the petition to the leaders of government. We hoped that Amnesty would take us seriously. And they did.

"After the petition was sent, it was clear that was not enough. The students decided to write more letters. But that was not enough, either."

The teacher passed out sheets of paper and asked the students to "think for five minutes. No talking. Let's just think. What else should we do?"

About six or seven of the returned papers said, "Build a school in Pakistan in Iqbal's memory." After reading the responses, a lightbulb went off in the students' heads. "That's it!" "That's it!" "Education, that's what he was telling us. Kids should be in school, not chained to looms." "That's it!"

Adams thought, Build a school in someone else's country . . . I don't think so. In the tiny towns and villages of South Asia, school is not an easy answer.

In spite of this view, Adams kept quiet. He didn't want to limit his students' dreams.

The students spun ideas off one another. Their first goal was to raise money and start a school in Iqbal's memory. Their second goal was to raise awareness. There were still millions of children in many countries who were forced to work in horrible conditions, the way Iqbal had worked.

Ideas were flying around the room. "We need our government to tell their government what we are going to do."

"We can't have people sending us money."

"Yeah, so we'll need a bank."

"And we need to get all kinds of kids involved in this."

They also said, "We need to work hand in hand with the Pakistanis. Otherwise, this would seem like a bunch of Americans coming in and telling them how they should be raising their children. That's not what we want. Let's build a friendship bridge with Pakistan."

All the experts agree that the most important step in the elimination of bonded child labor is education. But there are not enough schools to teach the large numbers of children, especially in the remote villages. To make this task even more difficult, UNICEF discovered that in many developing countries, the schools' curricula are "rigid and uninspiring." Many children say they would rather work and help their needy families than attend school and be bored or even mistreated.

None of this discouraged the students at Broad Meadows. Once their ideas were in place, they swung into action. The students stayed after school and sent e-mail messages to thirty-six middle schools in thirty-six states asking them to help. The Kids' Campaign to Build a School for Iqbal was born.

That night two students took it upon themselves to call local carpet stores and ask if they sold carpets made with child labor. They were cursed at and told to "mind their own business." The students concluded that the carpet merchants would not speak with them because it would affect their sales. Twelve-year-old Michael Gibbons called back. "You're wrong, Mr. Carpet Seller—this is everyone's business."

Two other students wrote a letter to Senator Kennedy, telling him what they were going to do and asking for his help. They also wrote to the mayor of their town to question the city's policy when buying carpets for municipal buildings.

The next morning the students rushed to school early. "Did we get anything?" "Did we get any answers on the net?" The teacher thought, Gosh, we just sent them out yesterday afternoon. He remained quiet. When the students went on-line, there were twelve responses, saying, "We're with you. . . . What can we do?"

The mayor, James Sheets, quickly replied to the students' questions. He said that there wasn't a policy regarding carpet purchases. There never had been a policy. But there would be one now!

Principal Anne Marie Zukauskas went to the bank and explained what the students were doing. The bank, a community bank, was only too helpful. They opened an account called the School for Iqbal.

Senator Kennedy issued a press statement saying that he supported the efforts to take a stand against child labor by building a school in Pakistan in memory of a former child bonded laborer named Iqbal Masih. Kennedy also acted as a government liaison and opened communications with the government of Pakistan. He arranged for the U.S. embassy in Pakistan to hand-deliver a letter to one of Prime Minister Bhutto's cabinet members. The letter explained what the children wanted to do. The reply, which wasn't in writing, consisted of four magical words: "We welcome your campaign."

That was it. The electronic human rights campaign to build a school for Iqbal was off and running—in three days.

Now it was up to the students to make the plan happen. They stayed late in school day after day, sending e-mail messages to other middle schools across the country, telling them what they were doing, telling

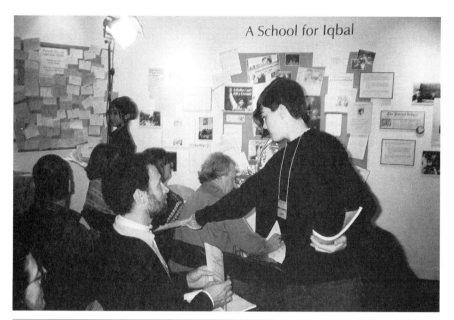

A School for Iqbal

them that Senator Kennedy and the government of Pakistan knew of this campaign and welcomed it and that there was a bank where they could send donations. Ron Adams said, "They asked the middle schools to learn more about child labor. If they wanted to become part of our campaign, here's how they could do it: either spread the word to another middle school or make a twelve-dollar donation to help us build a school." The twelve dollars was symbolic: it represented the amount of the loan that sold Iqbal into bonded labor and his age when he died.

Rick Roth, a representative from Amnesty International, helped them set up a web site:

> http://www.digitalrag.com/iqbal/index.html

Like ripples in a pond, word spread; one middle school told another middle school. Then another. Then another. Young people from all over the world logged on to the web site. They sent money and wrote letters to heads of state. To make money, they washed cars and held bake sales.

The principal at Broad Meadows allowed the students to turn the cafeteria into a command central. Every day before homeroom, they responded to the tons of mail that arrived from other schools. For one solid year the students wrote personal thank-you letters to everyone who sent in a donation. They had to do a separate fund-raiser just to pay for stamps.

After two years, three thousand schools and youth groups in all fifty states, as well as twenty-seven countries, became members of the campaign. At this writing, the students have raised more than $146,000. Twelve-dollar donations added up to $127,000. Reebok took the original $10,000 for Iqbal's education, added $2,000 more, and donated it to the project. Unions, and celebrities such as Jamie Lee Curtis, and Trudie Styler, as well as other concerned adults in twenty-four countries donated the rest.

Rock stars Michael Stipe of R.E.M. and Aerosmith sent letters to the school. Ron Adams said, "I couldn't help but notice the irony. Teenagers are getting fan mail from rock stars."

Once the students had the money, the question was, What to do with it?

They sent out a request for proposals to more than three hundred rights organizations that work for children. The students decided that a local Pakistani group called Sudhaar should become their partners because "they were most like us."

In Urdu, *sudhaar* means "enlightenment" or "improving." Sudhaar is a small, grassroots organization that is tied to the community. Its members know the problems of bonded children, and they have concrete ideas about solutions. They had already built a school for former bonded laborers and were respected in the human rights community. Most important, Sudhaar was respected in the Punjabi community where it was located, the same province where Iqbal was born, sold, and murdered.

Sudhaar got to work and began converting an office building into a School for Iqbal. Everyone pitched in. Members of the community donated their labor, materials, and money.

Doug Cahn, of the Reebok Foundation staff, visited the School for Iqbal when he was on a mission in Pakistan. He describes it: "I walked

105

A SCHOOL FOR IQBAL

down a narrow alley off a main, bustling, commercial street in Kasur. On either side of the alley were opened doorways where thread was being spun from wool. I couldn't help but observe child labor. It was everywhere I looked. There, in the middle of that kind of economy, in a culture that supports child labor and has done so for generations, exists this school.

"It exists because of the community support that the extraordinarily talented people in Pakistan were able to create and generate. It was just remarkable.

"I turned right and opened a door. There was the school. It was quite modest. There was a small office on the left, a courtyard, and four classrooms. Each of the classrooms was filled at different times of the day with different students, smiling children who were learning."

Sudhaar, under the leadership of Fawad Khan (no relation to Eshan Ullah Khan), is currently trying to educate the mothers. They want them to understand how education offers hope for their children. Even factory owners are making gradual changes.

Many of the schoolchildren are still bonded. But factory owners allow the child laborers to attend school. Instead of working fourteen hours a day, the children work eight to ten hours and then attend the school for two or three hours.

There is a large leather tannery near the school. The children work there and then go to school. At first their clothes were filthy from working in the factory. The school officials got the owners to install showers for the children. It was a small victory. But at least it was something.

Doug Cahn says, "The school not only represents hope for the three or four hundred kids who attend there, but it will act as a model, a kind of institution that can be replicated. That for me was a profound realization."

The Reebok Human Rights Foundation honored the Broad Meadows Middle School students with the Youth in Action Award. It was the same award that Iqbal had received.

Iqbal was an exceptional child, a real hero. He is an example of what one person can do for others by speaking out. He and his comrades show that people all around the world can work together to help bring about change.

Without the courage and dedication of Eshan Ullah Khan, Iqbal would never have been heard. Without the support of the international human rights community, the BLLF would have been crushed. Without the BLLF and human rights awards, Iqbal would never have met other children in Europe and America. Without the children in America, Iqbal's school would never have been built. Without a local group like Sudhaar, the School for Iqbal would never have worked. We must all help one another.

This book does not end here. Now it is our turn to stand up so that everyone can shout the words of Iqbal Masih: "We are free!"

Children Around the World Pick Up the Banner

When I was younger and eating steak with vegetables, Iqbal was working fourteen hours a day. When I was playing, Iqbal was still working. When I was watching TV, Iqbal was working harder and harder. He is free now, but there are still 7.5 million children in bonded labor right now in Pakistan. So when you get the chance, stop, maybe before bed or in the hall, while watching TV or when you are sitting on the bench waiting your turn to go into the game; think some. Turn off the TV or radio and pray, hope, and even later write a letter for the children of Pakistan.

I am more thankful, appreciative, and grateful. He made me think of easy and hard things in a different way.

—RICHARD KEEFE, A STUDENT AT BROAD MEADOWS MIDDLE SCHOOL

Sweden

Iqbal Masih touched the lives of many children around the world. In his quest to tell the world about child bondage, Iqbal spent a month in Lidköping, Sweden, a town of 25,000 people. Every schoolchild in Lidköping knew Iqbal. Some of them later visited him in Pakistan. After Iqbal's death, the Swedish schoolchildren formed two groups: Youth Against Slavery (YAS) and Children Against Slavery (CAS). On April 16, the students celebrate Iqbal Day in memory of their friend. Schools around the world are joining this celebration. The students are currently working to build the Iqbal Masih Freedom Centre for the Rights of the Child. For more information about Iqbal Day, visit the YAS web site at www.fredriksdalskolan.lidkoping.se.

Canada

In Canada, Craig Kielburger founded Free the Children International to give young people a voice on social issues and children's rights. His group promotes children's rights based on the United Nations Convention on the Rights of the Child. The web site is www.freethechildren.org.

Five Continents

At this writing plans are being made for a global march against child labor. In June 1998, representatives from around the world will meet in Geneva, Switzerland, where new international labor laws will be written and adopted at the International Labor Organization's Summit on Child Labor. At that time people will participate in a five-continent international march to support the end of child labor. The International Labor Rights Fund reports that the march "will focus on making sure that governments live up to the promises they have made in international declarations and conventions (most notably, the UN Convention on the Rights of the Child) and in their national constitution and laws."

"What about us?" questioned the student campaign leaders of the Kids' Campaign to Build a School for Iqbal. They asked the global march organizers to include children in their plans. As a result, the Robert F. Kennedy Memorial Center for Human Rights in Washington, DC, and other groups have created the Young People's Online March Against Child Labor, for those too young or unable to march. Each message posted will symbolize a mile marched against child labor by an individual, class, or youth group. Their e-mail address is endchlabor@aol.com.

Messages will be posted on Global March web site http://www.globalmarch.org.

Where to Learn More

Child Labor Resources on the World Wide Web

Ron Adams and the students of Broad Meadows Middle School graciously provided addresses and web sites to help you learn more about child labor. (If, in time, these web site addresses change, go into a server such as Yahoo or Alta Vista and search for the title of the organization you want to visit.)

Amnesty International USA
304 Pennsylvania Avenue, SE
Washington, DC 20003
Tel: 202/544-0200
Fax: 202/546-7142
http://www.amnesty.org

UNICEF Headquarters
3 UN Plaza
New York, NY 10017
Tel: 212/326-7000
Fax: 212/888-7465
http://www.unicef.org/aclabor/explore.htm

Child Labor Group
ILAB Room S, 1308
U.S. Department of Labor
Washington, DC 20210
http://www.dol.gov/dol/ilab/public/aboutilab/org/child.htm

Child Labor Coalition
1701 K Street
Washington, DC 20006
202/835-3323

American Federation of Teachers
International Affairs Department
555 New Jersey Avenue, NW
Washington, DC 20001-2079
http://www.aft.org//index.htm
Ask for a copy of *Child Labor: A Selection of Materials on Children in the Workplace.*

Human Rights Information on the Internet
http://www.igc.org/igc/issues/hr/or.html
This site lists many human rights groups.

Free the Children International
16 Thornbank Road
Thornhill, Ontario, Canada L4J 2A2
Tel: 905/881-0863
Fax: 905/881-1849
E-mail: freechild@clo.com
Web site: www.freethechildren.org

A School for Iqbal
Broad Meadows Middle School
50 Calvin Road
Quincy, MA 02169
http://www.digitalrag.com/iqbal/index.html

Other Addresses and Sites

Anti-Slavery International
The Stableyard
Broomgrove Road
London SW9 9TL England
Tel: 44171 924 9555
Fax: 44171 738 4110
http://www.charitynet.org/~asi

Bonded Labor Liberation Front (BLLF)
Västergatan 19
531 52 Lidköping, Sweden
Fax (BLLF Pakistan): 92-42-6316254
Fax (BLLF Sweden): 46-510-20599
E-mail: info@bllf.se
Web site: www.bllf.se

Children Against Slavery (CAS)
Stenhammarskolan
Brynåsavägen 5
531 56 Lidköping, Sweden
E-mail: stenhammarskolan@lidkoping.mail.telia.com

Child Workers in Nepal Concerned Centre
P.O. Box 4374
Kathmandu, Nepal
Tel: 97-71-270 336/271658
Fax: 97-71-270 336/224466

Human Rights Commission of Pakistan
Flat 13, Sharif Complex
Main Market
Gulberg II, Lahore, Pakistan
Tel: 92-42-5759219
Fax: 92-42-5713078

Human Rights Watch
350 Fifth Avenue
New York, NY 10118
Tel: 212/290-4700
Fax: 212/736-1300
E-mail: hrwnyc@hrw.org
Web site: http://www.hrw.org

International Labor Rights Fund
733 15th Street, NW
Suite 920
Washington, DC 20005
Tel: 202/347-4100
Fax: 202/347-4885
http://www.laborrights.com

National Child Labor Committee
1501 Broadway, Suite 1111
New York, NY 10036
Tel: 212/840-1801
Fax: 212/768-0963

South Asian Coalition on Child Servitude
Mukti Ashram
Ibrahimpur
Delhi 110036 India
Tel: 91-7202213
Fax: 91-3713355
E-mail: mukti@saccs.univ.ernet.in

Youth Against Slavery (YAS)
Fredriksdalskolan
Floragatan 4
531 36 Lidköping, Sweden
Fax: 46 510 83782
E-mail: yas.fredriksdalskolan@fredriksdalskolan.lidkoping.se
Web site: www.fredriksdalskolan.lidkoping.se

You Can Write to Iqbal's Family

Bonded Labor Liberation Front
1 Dysal Sing Mansion
The Mall
Lahore, Pakistan
Fax: 92-42-6316254

You Can Write to Heads of State

Prime Minister of Pakistan
Prime Minister House
Islamabad, Pakistan
Fax: 92-51-821835

President Rafiq Tarer
President House
Islamabad, Pakistan
Fax: 92-51-811390

You Can Write to United States Government Officials

The White House
1600 Pennsylvania Avenue
Washington, DC 20501
Tel: 202/456-1111
http://www.whitehouse.gov/WH/welcome.html

Check your local telephone book for the listing of your Congresspersons.

Notes

Complete information about the sources used is given in the bibliography, page 125.

Prologue

5–6   The quotation from the mother who sold her son into bondage comes from Molly Moore's article in the *International Herald Tribune* (22 May 1995), "Life Without Play for India's Child Laborers." I downloaded this material from an on-line information service, Lexis/Nexis; the page number of the quotation was not listed.

Chapter 1: My Name Is Iqbal

11   Iqbal's quote about working when he was four is reported in Trudie Styler's very personal article, "The Short, Tragic Life of Iqbal Masih," for *Harper's Bazaar*, February 1996. The Reebok Human Rights Foundation graciously provided a copy of this article, but the page number was not given.

15   The quotation from the mother that begins "When my children were three, . . ." is from Jonathan Silvers's fascinating article "Child Labor in Pakistan" in the February 1996 issue of the *Atlantic Monthly*, 82. This is a "must read" if you are interested in bonded child labor.

18   An account of nimble fingers comes from *The Small Hands of Slavery: Bonded Child Labor in India*, published by Human Rights Watch/Asia, 22. This report goes on to state that "nimble fingers" is both false and a rationalization.

Chapter 2: Carpet Weavers

20   For Iqbal's quote about being too afraid to help each other and most of his quotes in this chapter, see Styler. Iqbal repeated this statement to a number of journalists.

20   For children making errors, see Silvers, 83.

20   For "we often got lashed," see Jennifer Griffin, "Short and Heroic Life of Boy Who Was Sold for [160 Pounds] but Died for Nothing," [London] *Observer* (23 April 1995). This article was downloaded from Lexis/Nexis; page number was not listed.

21   Diseases suffered from inhaling wool comes from *Small Hands of Slavery,* 108.

21   For Iqbal's account of his experiences while in bondage, see Styler.

22   Additional accounts of the brutalities the bonded children face are reported in *Contemporary Forms of Slavery in Pakistan,* published by Human Rights Watch/Asia, 55.

23   For girls have a tougher time than boys, see *Small Hands of Slavery,* 16.

23, 25 Gauri Maya Taming, the carpet weaver in Kathmandu, describes her life as a carpet weaver in the Anti-Slavery International booklet by Omar Sattaur, *Child Labor in Nepal,* 35.

25   For Irfana's interview, see Silvers, 82.

26   Farhad Karim, a former researcher for Human Rights Watch/Asia, traveled throughout Pakistan and spoke with many bonded children. On July 4, 1997, I interviewed him in New York City. He told me about both his meeting with Iqbal and a harrowing visit with the carpet children of Thar. You can read more about these children in Human Rights Watch/Asia, *Contemporary Forms of Slavery,* 57.

27   *Contemporary Forms of Slavery* also depicts kidnapping, 53.

27–28 The account of the village barber who kidnapped a number of children is found in both *Small Hands of Slavery,* 105, and in Anti-Slavery International, "Slavery Today in India," Fact Sheet B, July 1994.

28   For the freeing of the children and the arrest of the barber, see Alan Whittaker, ed., *A Pattern of Slavery in India's Carpet Boys,* 5.

Chapter 3: Modern Forms of Slavery

Much of the research for this chapter evolved from readings and conversations with friends at Human Rights Watch/Asia and materials sent to me by Anti-Slavery International.

29   The quotation by Munirathna comes from *Small Hands of Slavery,* 61.

29–30 Ashiq's account of his life as a *beedi* roller can be found in Alan Whittaker, ed., *Children in Bondage: Slaves of the Subcontinent,* 19.

30   More information about the brick kilns comes from *Contemporary Forms of Slavery,* 44–45.

30   The price of the bricks sold in markets comes from both *Contemporary Forms of Slavery*, 36, and the Human Rights Commission of Pakistan, *The State of Human Rights, 1994* (Lahore: Human Rights Commission of Pakistan, 1994), 46.

31   The description by Sumathi and the number of *beedis* the older children are expected to roll come from *Small Hands of Slavery*, 47.

31   Powerful interviews of bonded children can be found in the UNICEF video *The State of the World's Children Report, 1997, Child Labour*. The testimonies from M. Velayulhan and M. Saritha come from that video.

31   To learn more about children sitting with matchboxes under their chins, see *Small Hands of Slavery*, 47.

33   Velayulhan's interview is from the UNICEF video, *The State of the World's Children Report*.

33–34 The young silversmiths are interviewed in *Small Hands of Slavery*, 67–68; Manojan's song is on 68.

34   For the quotation by Shabbir Jamal, see Silvers, 85.

34   For popular and false beliefs about children and work, see *Small Hands of Slavery*, 22 and 148. UNICEF has also described four myths in *The State of the World's Children, 1997* (New York: Oxford University Press, 1997). It states, "Child labor only happens in the poor world. . . . Child labor will never be eliminated until poverty disappears. . . . Child labor primarily occurs in export industries. . . . The only way to make a headway against child labor is for consumers and governments to apply pressure through sanctions and boycotts." This publication is another important source for anyone interested in child labor.

Chapter 4: Glass Houses

While I was doing research for this chapter, my colleague Russell Freedman introduced me to Jeffrey F. Newman, executive director of the National Child Labor Committee. Newman and his staff graciously gave me access to their files and provided Lewis Hine's inspiring photographs.

36   The description of the handbill can be found in a book edited by Robert H. Bremner, *Children and Youth in America: A Documentary History, 1866–1932*, vol. II (Cambridge: Harvard University Press, 1971), 616.

36–37 For Frederick K. Brown's poetic account of life in the spinning room, see Bremner, 616–19.

39   Lucy Larcom's childhood reflections are retold in editor Robert H. Bremner's *Children and Youth in America: A Documentary History, 1600–1865*, vol. I, 603–604. These fascinating books can be found in many libraries.

Chapter 5: "Jungle Fire"

Accurate reporting includes checking and rechecking one's sources. It is helpful when there is more than one source on a particular issue. Both Anti-Slavery International and Human Rights Watch provided the materials about Eshan Ullah Khan and about the NGOs that appear in this chapter. Then, just to make certain there were no mistakes, this section was e-mailed to BLLF members Britt-Marie Klang and Eshan Ullah Khan in Sweden to confirm the information.

41   For Eshan Ullah Khan's quote, see Marcus Harrison's *Eshan Ullah Khan: The Fight Against Slavery in Pakistan*, 25.

41–42 For the story of Baba Kullan, see Whittaker, *Children in Bondage*, 37–38.

42   Additional material about Eshan Ullah Khan comes from Harrison, 25 and 28.

42   Another source for information can be found in Human Rights Watch/Asia, *Contemporary Forms of Slavery*, 25.

44   Research about the Supreme Court abolishing debt bondage and the *peshgi* system comes from *Children in Bondage*, 40, and *Contemporary Forms of Slavery*, 27.

45   The investigations into conditions in small villages in India is reported in *Children in Bondage*, 40.

45   The quotation about Ashram Mukyi and the slavery syndrome is from Sydney H. Schanberg's "Six Cents an Hour," in *Life* (June 1996), 38.

45–47 An account of the 1989 seminar with bonded children in New Delhi and the testimony of Manga Masih, a brick kiln worker, can be found in *Children in Bondage*, 39.

47   *Children in Bondage* furnishes the testimony of Sita Lakshmi, a match and fireworks maker, 12.

47   The quotation by the stone cutter, Baleka, is in *Children in Bondage*, 14.

48   The Convention on the Rights of the Child, 1989, is one of the most important human rights documents ever written. The following three articles are especially relevant for the bonded child laborer: Article 32 states that parties recognize the right of the child to be protected from economic exploitation and from performing any work that is likely to be hazardous or harmful to the child's health or physical, mental, spiritual, moral, or social development. Article 35 states that parties shall take all appropriate measures to prevent the abduction and sale of children for any purpose or in any form. Article 36 states that parties shall protect the child against all other forms of exploitation prejudicial to any aspects of the child's welfare. See *Small Hands of Slavery*, 26, and *Children in Bondage*, 64. For information about the Convention on the Rights of the Child, contact the United Nations, UNICEF, or visit their web site (http://www.unicef.org/crc/conven.htm).

49   For more about "carpet looms . . . in every nook and cranny," see *Small Hands of Slavery*, 112. Some of the material for this chapter comes from conversations with Arvind Ganesan, a Human Rights Watch researcher who worked on *Small Hands of Slavery*.

49   Laxmi's quote can be found in *Small Hands of Slavery*, 112–13.

50   The investigation about police accountability is described in *Contemporary Forms of Slavery*, 68.

Chapter 6: We Demand an End to Slavery

51   Iqbal's quote about his parents being helpless can be found in Styler.

51   Journalist Mark Schapiro visited with Iqbal's mother and sister in Lahore for his article "Children of a Lesser God." He later talked with me about what he learned of Iqbal's student years.

53   The spokesman's denial to charges made by Eshan Ullah Khan can be found in the article by Tim Kelsey, "Fight to Rescue Pakistani Child Slaves," in *The Independent* (14 August 1991), 10.

Chapter 7: Certificate of Freedom

56   For "He sat cowering," see Ivy George, "A Brief Sojourn, A Lasting Legacy," *Brandeis Review*, 50. The Reebok Foundation sent me a copy of this article; the date was not given.

56   For research about what happens when some person challenges the law, see *Small Hands of Slavery*, 21.

56–58 The work done by the BLLF in Pakistan, reactions, and the *Charter of Freedom* can be found in Silvers, 85. This material was reviewed for accuracy by Eshan Ullah Khan and Britt-Marie Klang.

58   For the response, "What is the alternative for these poor children?" see Moore, "Life Without Play for India's Child Laborers."

58   Iqbal's "My owner threatened me" recounting is from *MTV's Get Up, Stand Up: The Fight for Human Rights*, first broadcast March 26, 1997.

58   For Eshan Ullah Khan's "I brought him on stage," see Griffin.

59   Iqbal's "Come with me and be free" quote is in "Breaking the Chains," *Scholastic Scope* 44, no. 13 (9 February 1996), 13.

Chapter 8: Action

63   For Senator Harkin's comment about products made by child labor, see Onapito-Ekomoloit, "U.S.—Children: New Bill Would Ban Child-Labor Imports," Inter Press Service (19 July 1995). This article was downloaded from Lexis/Nexis; no page number listed.

63 Much of the reporting of Senator Tom Harkin's reaction to bonded labor comes from an article by Julie Naughton, "Harkin Child-Labor Bill Adds Senate Resolution," *HFD, The Weekly Home Furnishings Newspaper* 67, no. 43 (25 October 1993), 23. This material was downloaded from Lexis/Nexis.

64 Beauty's account of her work in a Bangladesh garment factory is portrayed in the UNICEF video, *The State of the World's Children Report, 1997.*

64 The response by an employer is found in an article by Sabir Mustafa, "Dateline: Dhaka, Bangladesh," UPI (17 January 1993). This article, downloaded from Lexis/Nexis, did not have a page number.

65 Sulfa's quote comes from the UNICEF video.

65 For the research beginning "Many children found jobs," see *The State of the World's Children, 1997*, 60.

65 For "When my children cry for food, . . ." see "Dateline: Dhaka, Bangladesh."

65 The way governments and grassroots organizations are addressing this problem is discussed in the video *The State of the World's Children Report, 1997.*

66–67 When I interviewed Doug Cahn, he told me about meeting Eshan Ullah Khan.

Chapter 9: A Proper Schoolboy . . . and Activist

Once Iqbal was in school, he began meeting international researchers and the press. I learned about Iqbal's school days in interviews with Farhad Karim of Human Rights Watch/Asia; Mark Schapiro, the journalist; and Doug Cahn of the Reebok Human Rights Foundation who helped bring Iqbal to America.

Rugmark was researched with the help of UNICEF, the International Labor Rights Fund, and Anti-Slavery International. Pharis Harvey, the president of Rugmark Foundation, U.S.A., graciously provided additional material and gave us permission to use the Rugmark logo.

Chapter 10: Just Like Abraham Lincoln

This chapter was created from a series of interviews with Sharon Cohen, Paula Van Gelder, and Doug Cahn, of the Reebok Human Rights Foundation, and with Ron Adams, a teacher at the Broad Meadows Middle School where Iqbal visited. It was then reviewed for accuracy by the Reebok staff and by Ron Adams and his students.

Chapter 11: Return to Pakistan

The account and testimonies about Iqbal's murder are provided by the Human Rights Commission of Pakistan. They generously sent me a great deal of background material, including a copy of "Murder of Iqbal Masih: HRCP Report," July 1995. For that report, their representatives conducted a fact-finding mission. They interviewed Amanat Masih, Iqbal's maternal uncle; Hidayat Masih, father of an eyewitness; Inayat Bibi, Iqbal's mother; neighbors; Ashraf Hero, the accused murderer; Ali Hussain, Ashraf's employer; the police; and carpet manufacturers.

88 For quotation by I. A. Rehman, see Silvers, 91.

91 For honoring Iqbal, see Kathy Gannon, "Killing of Pakistan's Boy Activist Draws Demands for Banning of Child Labour," [London] *Guardian* (21 April 1995), 16.

91–92 The Reebok Human Rights Foundation sent the entire speech in which Khan asked consumers and exporters to say no to child labor. This speech was given soon after Iqbal's death to the UN Working Group on Contemporary Forms of Slavery.

Chapter 12: Who Killed Iqbal Masih?

Many of the quotations, background material, and testimony by Iqbal's murderer come from the fact-finding mission of the Human Rights Commission of Pakistan.

95 For "Never before have we had so many people . . ." see Farhan Bokhari, "Pakistan to Crack Down on Child Labour," *Financial Times* (18 July 1996), 4.

95 From "Pakistan Open to Examination of Child Murder," Agence France Presse, International News (2 July 1995). This material was downloaded from Lexis/Nexis; the byline and page number were not listed.

95 For action against the BLLF, see Silvers, 92.

96 For the creation of a trust fund, see Human Rights Watch/Asia, *Bonded Labor Update, A Human Rights Watch Short Report* I, no. 1 (July 1997).

Chapter 13: A School for Iqbal

This chapter is mostly based on a long interview with Ron Adams, the teacher at the Broad Meadows Middle School. Soon thereafter Doug Cahn told me his impressions following his visit to the School for Iqbal in Pakistan.

99 Student Didier Alther's quotation is on the School for Iqbal web site, and is used with the permission of the students at the Broad Meadows Middle School. More students' reactions to Iqbal's death can be found on the Internet: http://www.digitalrag.com/iqbal/index.html

104 For ". . . Teenagers are getting fan mail . . . ," see "Breaking the Chains," *Scholastic Scope* 44, no. 13 (9 February 1996), 14.

Glossary and Pronunciation Guide

Words in *italics* are from the Urdu or Hindi languages. This is an informal pronunciation guide; the actual sound of each word may vary greatly from place to place.

beedi (bee di).   A cheap cigarette.

bhatta (bha tha; the *bh* is almost like a cough).   Site or workplace.

bibi (bee bee).   Dear woman.

charpay (chaar pay).   A bed or platform made of hemp.

chowkidar (chou ki dar).   A guard or overseer.

dera (dey rah).   A meeting place.

Iqbal Masih (ik bal mah see).

katcha (kah cha, like "gotcha").   Raw or unpaved.

mule room.   Spinning room.

mules.   Machinery.

naksha (nak shah).   A map or pattern.

nongovernmental organizations.   Independent groups of activists.

pathera (pah terah).   A person who works with wet clay in the brick kiln.

peshgi (pey shee).   A loan.

roti (rou tey).   Indian flat bread.

rupee.   A unit of money.

shalwaar kamiz (shal var kah meeze).   Baggy cotton trousers and long shirt, traditional dress in Pakistan.

sudhaar (sud haar).   Enlightenment or improving.

thekedar (tay kay dar).   An employer or boss.

ustaad (oo stahd).   Teacher.

Bibliography

These books and articles were particularly helpful in my learning more about child bondage:

Bokhari, Farhan. "Pakistan to Crack Down on Child Labour." *Financial Times* (18 July 1996).

Freedman, Russell. *Kids at Work: Lewis Hine and the Crusade Against Child Labor.* New York: Clarion Books, 1994.

Harrison, Marcus. *Eshan Ullah Khan: The Fight Against Slavery in Pakistan.* Anti-Slavery International Report, 1991.

Human Rights Commission of Pakistan. *Bonded Haris of Sindh.* Lahore, 1996.

———. *Camel Kids Revisited, 1992–93.* Lahore, 1993.

———. *State of Human Rights in 1996.* Lahore, 1996.

Human Rights Watch/Asia. *Contemporary Forms of Slavery in Pakistan.* New York, 1995.

———. *The Small Hands of Slavery: Bonded Child Labor in India.* New York, 1996.

Human Rights Watch/Asia and Children's Rights Project. *Police Abuse and Killings of Street Children in India.* New York, 1996.

Kruijtbosch, Martine. *Rugmark: A Brief Resume of Concept to Reality for Visual Guarantee of Carpets Made Without Child Labour.* New Delhi: South Asian Coalition on Child Servitude, 1996.

Kuklin, Susan. *Irrepressible Spirit: Conversations with Human Rights Activists.* New York: Putnam, 1996.

Meltzer, Milton. *Cheap Raw Material: How Our Youngest Workers Are Exploited and Abused.* New York: Viking, 1994.

Moore, Molly. "Life Without Play for India's Child Laborers: Sold into Servitude/ Youngsters in the Workplace." *International Herald Tribune* (22 May 1995).

Parker, David. *Stolen Dreams.* Minneapolis: Lerner Publications, 1998.

Pradhan, Gauri. "Child Workers in the Carpet Factories of Nepal." *Voice of Child Workers* (December 1992): 24–36.

Sattaur, Omar. *Child Labor in Nepal.* Kathmandu: Anti-Slavery International and Child Workers in Nepal Concerned Centre, 1993.

Satyarthi, Kailash. *Break the Chains, Save the Childhood.* Delhi: South Asian Coalition on Child Servitude, 1994.

Schanberg, Sydney H. "Six Cents an Hour." *Life* (June 1996): 38–46.

Schapiro, Mark. "Children of a Lesser God." *Harper's Bazaar* (April 1996).

Selden, Bernice. *The Mill Girls.* New York: Atheneum, 1983.

Silvers, Jonathan. "Child Labor in Pakistan." *Atlantic Monthly* (February 1996): 79–92.

Springer, Jane. *Listen to Us.* Toronto: Groundwood Books, 1997.

Styler, Trudie. "The Short, Tragic Life of Iqbal Masih." *Harper's Bazaar* (February 1996).

UNICEF. *The State of the World's Children, 1997.* New York: Oxford University Press, 1997.

Whittaker, Alan, ed. *A Pattern of Slavery in India's Carpet Boys.* London: Anti-Slavery International, 1988.

———. *Children in Bondage: Slaves of the Subcontinent.* Child Labor Series, no. 10. London: Anti-Slavery International, 1989.

Index

128
―――――――
IQBAL MASIH AND
THE CRUSADERS
AGAINST CHILD
SLAVERY

"Talk back" boys, 21
Taming, Gauri Maya, 23–25, *24*, 28
Thar, Pakistan, carpet children of,
    26–27
Thekedars, 13–14, 15, 16, 20, 21, 26
Toys, child workers in making of, 5
Tuberculosis, 21, 26

Underwood, Blair, 84–85, *85*
UNICEF. *See* United Nations Interna-
    tional Children's Emergency
    Fund
United Nations, 84
United Nations Convention on the Rights
    of the Child, 48, 49, 109, 110
United Nations Human Rights Com-
    mission (UNHRC), 53–55, 66,
    71, 91–92
United Nations Human Rights confer-
    ence (1993), 65–67
United Nations International Children's
    Emergency Fund (UNICEF), 5,
    7, 31, 33, 53, 64, 65, 66, 71,
    101, 111
United States
    activism in, 38, 39–40, 63–64,
        99–106

child labor in, 34–40, *37–39*
labor laws in, 38
products made by child labor
    banned in, 63–64, 96
slavery in, 14, 69, 79, 80
writing to government officials in,
    114

Van Gelder, Paula, 75, 79–80, 82, 83,
    86, 94
Velayulhan, M., 33

Wages, of child workers, 20, 23–25,
    30, 33
Watching agents, 16
Weaving looms, *17*, 17–18
    see also Carpet weavers
Web sites, 103, 109, 110, 111–14
Weddings, loans taken for, 13

Young People's Online March Against
    Child Labor, 110
Youth Against Slavery (YAS), 109,
    114

Zia ul Haq, General, 49
Zukauskas, Anne Marie, 102